WAGING WAR ON REAL ESTATE'S DISCOUNTERS

How to Unlock the Door to a Full Commission

Bernice L. Ross, Ph.D

Published in the United States of America by
Teleclass4U.com, LLC
P.O. Box 90849
Austin, TX 78709-0849
(512) 301-1644

Cover Design: Klingsmith & Company

First edition published February 2005

The Library of Congress Cataloging-in-Publication Data Applied For

Ross, Bernice L.
Waging War on Real Estate's Discounters:
How to Unlock the Door to a Full Commission

ISBN: 0-9763243-0-X

*To my family who have helped to make me all
I am today—to my brother Vernon Ross and
in loving memory of my parents
Alma P. and H.B. Ross*

Contents

Acknowledgements

I am extremely grateful to our wonderful clients and readers for their continued support of our products and services. I would also like to express my sincere appreciation to each of the following people who contributed to the creation of this book.

Shane Bowlin, virtual assistant extraordinaire, has guided this entire effort from start to finish including laying out the final manuscript, proofing, locating our graphics artist, overseeing the work with our publisher, coordinating the website design, marketing, and a host of other tasks to numerous to list. Without her wisdom and expertise, this project would never have come into being.

Special thanks to my editor Judy Kleinberg. Her writing and editorial skills substantially upgraded the quality of this book. Judy is a tremendously talented editor, free-lance writer, as well as the co-author of *Fat, Stupid, Ugly: One Woman's Courage to Survive*.

Brad Inman, Publisher of *Inman News* and founder of HomeGain, graciously agreed to write the foreword for this book. I am honored to be one of Brad's weekly columnists and am grateful to him and the entire Inman News team for publishing my articles. I am also grateful to everyone at HomeGain for their assistance in helping me understand the many facets of the lead generation business.

I especially appreciate each of the editors I have worked with over the last four years. Jessica Sweesey, the Editor of *Inman News,* created the title for this book. She changed the original title for my articles on discounting from *Defending Your Commission* to *Waging War on Real Estate's Discounters.* Marcie Geffner, the former editor of *Inman News,* and Blanche Evans, Editor of *Realty Times*, both helped me to grow as a writer. Blanche also introduced me to Alexa.com as an independent source to track web activity.

I am indebted to Cheryl Klinginsmith of Klinginsmith & Company for the brilliant cover for *Waging War.* She took my comments about the topic and turned it into a cover that far exceeded my expectations.

A special thanks to Alex Periello, President and Chief Executive Officer, Cendant Real Estate, for his encouragement to write this book. When my articles first appeared in *Inman News,* Alex's feedback motivated me to develop this topic into a full-blown book.

I deeply appreciate the contributions of each of the following agents who shared their strategies for earning a full commission: Craig Ashley, Tim Burrell, Gail Crann, Michael Edlen, Ginny Hillenbrand, Lee Konowe, Jackie

Leavenworth, Lucy Matsumoto, Shawne Mitchell, Jerry Rossi, Nancy Sanborn, BarbaraVan Stensel, and Adrian Willanger.

Special thanks to Gary Keller, Dave Jenks, and Jay Papasan, best selling authors of the *Millionaire Real Estate Agent*, for their inspiration and guidance. I am indebted to Gary for the opportunity to work with the very talented KWU instructional design team led by Mary Weaver. The agent interviews are a direct result of Gary's recommendation that sharing stories from agents "makes the material come alive."

Robert Brand, Randy Lowry, Steve Schwartz, and Don Sherwood helped me gain a better understanding of disclosure issues. Their input was critical to the chapter on risk management.

Janet Choynowski of Immobel.com provided the information on how to market globally using their service that translates Multiple Listing Service data into twelve different languages.

Albert Clark of MyHomeManagementClub.com has spent hours educating me on how to best use an e-mail newsletter to attract, track, and then convert leads into signed business.

Marc Davison of VREO Software has been conducting focus groups examining the best strategies for converting real estate website visitors into clients. Many of the suggestions contained in the Internet marketing chapters are based upon VREO's findings. I admire Marc's dedication to helping agents match the needs of consumers and am especially grateful to Marc for recommending me as a columnist for *Inman News*.

Thanks to Gary Elwood and Rick Owens of Proquest Technologies for sharing their research on how an 800 Call Capture system increases lead generation rates as well as for sharing their strategies on how to incorporate call capture into listing presentations.

Jim Gilreath uses the concept of competitor reconnaissance in his recruiting and retention training for managers. I adapted Jim's concept for agents to use during their listing presentations. I deeply appreciate Jim's encouragement to put our training on audio CD, his assistance in that process, and for his encouragement along the way.

Tim Johnson, Adam Pascu, and the rest of the team at Z57.com were responsible for the design of the current RealEstateCoach.com website. Adam mentored me on using pay-per-click services and provided much of the information for that chapter. Z57 also shared their internal research on what web visitors click on when they visit a real estate website.

Special thanks to Josh and Lee Konowe of E-Agent.biz. In addition to helping me locate some of the best agents in the business for interviews, Josh mentored me on the intricacies of achieving excellent search engine ranking and using their lead generation service to convert web leads into signed business. Along with his father Lee, they also provided the bulk of the information on how to market using cable television and radio.

Donna Lauer of UniqueGlobalEstates.com provided the strategies outlining how estates agents can market their million-dollar-plus listings to international buyers using the web.

Thanks to Rich May and the rest of the Coldwell Banker educational team for their steadfast support since 1998, for their assistance in creating our coaching team, and for sharing my articles on the Coldwell Banker intranet site each week.

Jack Peckham of RECyber.com is a fount of wisdom on the subject of real estate technology. Jack's monthly interviews and RECyber's annual on-line convention consistently help me stay up-to-date with the latest trends and new technology tools.

Michael Russer created the concept of being client-centric rather than agent-centric. Michael's client-centric approach is at the heart of providing superb customer service.

I am grateful to the National Association of Realtors —their ethical guidelines were a critical piece of this book.

To my friends and colleagues from the former Jon Douglas Company, thanks for a 17-year run of being "the best in the business." Special thanks to Jack Douglas for his leadership in setting the bar of professionalism so high, his commitment to always doing the right thing for the customer, and for the honor of being the Executive Director of Training for his company for five years. JDCO was fondly known as the "Rolls Royce of Realtors." I hope this book conveys the standard of excellence Jack sought to create.

Thanks also to Lou Piatt, Diana Brookes, Fran Flanagan, Randy Forbes, Betty Graham, Jon Greenleaf, Lori Hawkins, Peter Hernandez, Laura Lee Anthony, Tom Dunlap, and to all the other members of the former JDCO management team. I am also grateful to all the talented trainers I have worked with in the past including Wanda Bolint, Cathy Brown, Carol Ellis, Dawn Evans, Cynthia Freeman, Karen Greensweig, Stan (Stock) Jonekos, Nancy Plotkin, Gaye Rainey, Nancy Sanborn, and the late Ray Haddad. Each of them helped me grow as both a businessperson and a trainer. Their shared wisdom appears throughout this book.

RealEstateCoach.com would not exist without our talented team of real estate coaches who have provided coaching services to our clients since 1999. David Brown, Christine D'Amico, Joeann Fossland, Ginger Jenks, Patti Kaprellian, Judy Lowry, Cork Motsett, Alvah Parker, Sharon Teitelbaum, Jeff Thompson, Jim Vuoculo, and Gary Wood, each of you is a gift to the clients you serve as well as the entire real estate industry.

RealEstateCoach.com relies upon a number of companies who make it possible to deliver our products to our clients. Special thanks to Darlene Lyons of Broker Agent Speaker's Bureau who handles my speaking engagements; David Behrens and Brian Wildermuth of Sharper Agent (contact management and marketing); Dick Maney of Maney Telefilm (sound engineer and audio CD recording); Kim Ades and Igor Kotlyar of Upward Motion for the Real Estate Simulator Assessment; Marty Crouch of Web Valence (web hosting, newsletter distribution, and spam slayer); James Komosinski of Practice Pay Solutions (merchant services); Sylvia Tooker of Bear Data (web design); National Media (audio CD production); Fidlar Doubleday (printing); and to our publisher Teleclass4U.com, LLC.

A heartfelt thanks to the very special coaches/mentors who have helped me on my personal journey including Marilyn Naylor, Meryl Moritz, Karen Whitworth, and the late Thomas Leonard.

And most of important of all, Byron Van Arsdale, my husband, partner, coach, and best friend—thank you for keeping me laughing and writing, even on the days when I felt like crying.

Foreword

by Bradley Inman
Founder and Publisher of *Inman News*

Real estate commissions are under siege. The Internet, the rise of alternative business models, and the shortage of home listings have conspired to make the full-service real estate commission as antiquated as the typewriter.

These trends are not daunting to writer, author, and real estate expert Bernice Ross. In her new book, *Waging War on Real Estate's Discounters*, Ross maps a path for preserving the full-service commission. Ross, a gifted communicator, peels back the onion on the issue giving a clear and cogent argument as to why the notion of reduced commissions has been popularized in the last few years. Ross does not blame the innovators, the Internet, or the discounters. Instead, she offers an alternative path for her full-service peers who may be intimidated by the current environment and may feel pressured by the shortage of home listings in the marketplace.

Most importantly, Ross offers a convincing formula for insuring reduced commissions do not tempt sellers, starting with bolstering the confidence of Realtors® themselves when they pitch new listings. Her step-by-step guide shows full service Realtors® how to overcome what Ross terms the Big Lie: reducing the broker's commission nets more money for the seller.

Waging War on Real Estate's Discounters is exactly what every capable Realtor® should follow if they are seriously interested in preserving their business and standing head and shoulders above the crowd.

Introduction
Battling THE Big Lie:
Reducing the Broker's Commission
Nets More Money for the Seller

We must all wage an intense, lifelong battle against the constant downward pull. If we relax, the bugs and weeds of negativity will move into the garden and take away everything of value.
— Jim Rohn

Are you tired of seeing your commissions eroded by discounters? Are you going to sit there and continue to take it or are you ready to "Wage War on Real Estate's Discounters?" If you're tired of having to defend your commission at every turn, then it's time to reclaim your power and start earning the full commissions you deserve.

Make no mistake about it. You are at war. The enemy, however, isn't just the poorly trained agent in your office or down the street. It's billion dollar companies who now see your commissions as fair game in this all-out battle. Like defenseless little lambs, agents have given the enemy the perfect opportunity to seize a huge piece of our territory. Instead of fighting back, many agents are running in fear.

When you know how hard you work for your clients, doesn't it make you angry when you hear, "You earn too much in commission?" The truth of the matter is your clients are willing to pay a full commission, provided they see a benefit in doing so. The reason so many agents surrender part of their commission is they are unable to explain the value they bring to the transaction. Changing this trend will require you to create tremendous value for your clients while simultaneously providing an extraordinary customer service experience.

If you think this book is going to blame discounters for our problems, you're sadly mistaken. Many agents and companies complain about lead aggregators, limited service brokers, or on-line discounters. It's time to realize this war must be fought elsewhere. To win, we must first win the battle with ourselves. Winning also will require in-depth competitor reconnaissance, innovative strategies, and swift, decisive action.

Waging War is about reaching your own personal pinnacle of excellence. As Stephen Covey contends: "Trying to do well and trying to beat others are two different things. Excellence and victory are conceptually different and are experienced differently."

As Covey correctly observes, winning and excellence are entirely different. When you focus on beating the competition, you lose. To effectively wage war on discounters, you must shift your win-lose approach to making it a win-win for the consumer.

When you focus on providing excellent service and meeting your clients' needs, the win-lose aspect disappears. No matter what you do, some clients will always select their agent based upon who has the lowest commission. Winning agents recognize this and honor the client's decision. Most clients, however, want excellent value and are willing to pay for it. As Ralph Waldo Emerson observed, "If a man has good corn, or wood, or boards, or pigs to sell, or can make better chairs or knives, crucibles, or church organs, than anybody else, you will find a broad, hard-beaten road to his house, though it be in the woods."

Although excellence and customer service are the cornerstones of earning a full commission, they are not enough. Ries and Trout in their book, *Marketing Warfare* (1986), point out a new trend that started in the 1980s and is being played out today in both traditional and web-based marketing venues: "The true nature of marketing today is not serving the customer; it is outwitting, outflanking, out fighting your competitors. In short, marketing is the war where the enemy is the competition and the customer is the ground to be won."

Rather than battling consumers for our commission, the real objective is to win the consumer. Winning requires being the absolute best you can be. In fact, the better you are, the fewer battles you will fight. Furthermore, excellence attracts a higher quality client who seeks the superb service you provide. This in turn leads to a long-term sustainable business where referrals are easy to generate.

Winning the consumer requires you to attack "The Big Lie." What is the Big Lie? It's the lie that reducing the commission always results in more money for the seller. Nothing could be further from the truth.

Virtually all sellers want to obtain the highest price possible for their property. As an agent, you have a fiduciary duty to help sellers obtain this important goal. No matter what you are selling, maximum exposure to the marketplace is the critical factor in achieving the highest price possible. Companies and agents who cut services in exchange for taking a lower commission often cost clients much more than the extra one to three percent they save in commission. Depending on price, the cost can be tens of thousands of dollars.

Waging War on Real Estate's Discounters attacks the Big Lie on a number of fronts. The stakes in this war are high. Our foes are no longer the agents or brokerage down the street. They're well-funded billion dollar giants who are determined to capture our clients and our commissions. These fierce challengers understand how to drive sales using their own business relationships while also capitalizing on today's web-based marketing environment. To win the war in this new hyper-competitive market, you can no longer afford to be reactive in your marketing and prospecting efforts. Instead, you must take the initiative and start thinking about your business as if your rival is one of these major corporations. Like it or not, this is the war you must fight.

The purpose of this book is simple:
To provide you with a comprehensive "Waging War" battle plan that uses technology, competitor reconnaissance, and guerilla marketing strategies to differentiate your high quality services from your competitors and thus convert your clients into raving fans.

To wage war successfully, you must fight the battle for the consumer on two fronts. First, you must defend against competitors. The most important battle, however, will be the one you wage to reach your personal best in terms of professionalism, customer service, and value to the consumer.

Waging War provides the ammunition you need to win on both fronts. Whether you win or lose is up to you. The strategies you're about to learn work—provided you put forth the time and effort to plan, master, and execute what this book covers. If you're ready to win the consumer, then it's time to create a plan of attack.

Preparation

Do not wait; the time will never be "just right." Start where you stand, and work with whatever tools you may have at your command...Better tools will be found as you go along.

—Napoleon Hill

Chapter 1
Survey the Battlefield

The battlefield is a scene of constant chaos.
The winner will be the one who controls that chaos,
both his own and that of his enemy.
— Napoleon Bonaparte

As an individual agent, how can you compete with huge companies and major real estate brands that discount? There are two primary strategies. Since most people are willing to pay for top-notch service, the first strategy is to become the Rolls Royce of Realtors®. The second strategy, according to Ries and Trout (1986), is to become a guerrilla marketer. Thousands of local real estate companies use guerrilla tactics to compete successfully against major national brands. Their strategy is simple: stay small, own a specific market niche, and offer services major competitors do not provide. You can apply the same strategy whether competing against a discounter or a major competitor down the street. Carve out a specific niche where you are the expert. Big companies cannot and will not compete for small pieces of the market. Provide services your competitors do not provide and be able to articulate the benefits of those services to your clientele.

Customize Your Battle Plan

Winning the war requires a battle plan. Your primary objective is to assist sellers in achieving the highest price for their property in the shortest amount of time. To achieve this goal, the sellers' property must have maximum exposure to the marketplace. The greater the exposure, the more likely the sellers are to achieve the highest possible price. Consequently, you must be able to articulate how your services help the sellers achieve this important goal.

Like any battle, the more carefully you prepare, the more likely you are to succeed. The steps you must take to win the consumer are below.

Part 1: Start with Yourself: Winning the Psychological War

To create a successful waging war marketing campaign, you must first identify your personal Unique Selling Proposition (USP).

What makes you unique?
To begin this process, determine the specific qualities that differentiate you from other salespeople. Some examples of unique agent branding include the Hat Lady, the Tuxedo Realtor®, and the Real Estate Doctor. Your goal is to recognize what makes you special and then identify how that benefits your clientele.

What's your niche?
A second important part of your USP is developing specific niches you service. For example, if you have a teaching background, consider developing a niche representing teachers. If you are passionate about golf or boating, work on creating a niche that services people who share your passion. Other niches can include your local neighborhood, your place of worship, or specific market segments such as estates, probates, or relocation.

Determine what Waging War strategies you already use.
As you read through the subsequent chapters, identify the services you already provide. These services represent the battle preparations you have already completed.

Identify new approaches to gain both a strategic and tactical advantage.
While it is important to identify services you already provide, adding three to five services your competitors do not provide can create a huge competitive advantage. In fact, to win the consumer and to overcome the discount objection, approach each chapter with two different thoughts in mind. First, will this strategy create a competitive advantage? Second, is this strategy something you would feel comfortable using on a regular basis? As you read each chapter, always keep these two important criteria in mind.

Part 2: Plan Your Waging War Marketing Campaign

The Waging War Marketing Campaign consists of four different parts.

1. *The agent campaign*

   Since the large majority of properties sell through other agents, marketing to the agent community is pivotal to helping the seller achieve the highest price possible in the shortest time.

2. *The public campaign*

   The public part of your Waging War Marketing Campaign includes strategies for marketing to the public, including 800 Call Capture (Interactive Voice Recognition or IVR technology), traditional mailings, open houses, customized marketing materials, cable television, and radio.

3. *The web campaign*

   Web marketing reaches both the public and other agents. You need strategies to reach buyers locally, nationally, and internationally. *Waging War* provides specific strategies for winning Internet buyers and sellers.

4. *The customer service campaign*

   Everyone talks about customer service. Few have a strategy to implement customer service as a powerful weapon in their listing consultation arsenal.

The Waging War Marketing Campaign is extensive. You may be wondering if you need this huge arsenal to win over the seller. Sometimes a simple script is all you need. In other cases, you will need every item in your arsenal. The better the job you do in marketing the property, the more likely you are to sell it. Extensive marketing pleases the seller. From your perspective, these strategies shorten market time. This means waging a smart marketing battle right from the beginning will make you more money with less effort. Consequently, as you read through the chapters outlining the marketing portions of your campaign, note which tactics best suit your marketplace and your style of doing business.

Part 3: Competitor Reconnaissance

When properly executed, competitor reconnaissance creates a tremendous competitive edge. There are three steps.

1. *Do the numbers*

   This is an on-going process, one you must track consistently. The goal is to show sellers how listing at a full commission actually nets them more money in most cases. To demonstrate this, you must collect Multiple Listing Service (MLS) data on each of your competitors and compare it to your personal or company market statistics.

2. *Risk management*

   Most agents cringe when they hear these words, yet a well-articulated risk management program is one of the easiest ways to differentiate your services from your competitors. This is effective against all competitors, not just discounters.

3. *Select a battle plan*

   To win the war, you must know what your competitors are doing. What services do they provide? What is their plan of attack? What do you do that is different? To answer these questions you must do your research and then clearly present the differences to the seller. Waging War outlines two distinct Battle Plans for differentiating your services from those of your competitors. No matter what method you select, your USP is your best defense against discount attacks.

Part 4: The Waging War Listing Consultation

Ultimately, you will win or lose this battle during your listing consultation. If not well executed, even an excellent plan can result in failure. The Waging War listing consultation prepares you to deliver a crushing blow to agents in your own office who cut commissions, to limited service brokerages who discount, as well to on-line discount competitors.

Part 5: Working with Buyers, Defending Your Turf, and the Attraction A-Bomb

Finally, *Waging War* also examines some simple strategies to obtain full commissions when you work with buyers as well as how to defend your commission once you place a property under contract.

An Important Caveat:
DO NOT OVER-PROMISE!

The strategies in *Waging War* are extremely effective provided you do what you tell the seller you will do. If you fail to fulfill a promise, however, you have misrepresented your services. This destroys the seller's trust. It also opens the door for the seller to discount your commission, or worse, terminate your listing.

To avoid this trap, a great rule to remember is to under-promise and over-deliver. This means offering the seller about 75 percent of what you think you can complete, and then providing more services than you promised.

How to Use this Book

At the beginning of each chapter, you will find a list of strategies the chapter covers. To make the best use of this book, follow the guidelines below:

1. Before reading the chapter, note the items listed at the beginning of the chapter and put a check mark (√) next to the strategies you already use.

2. Throughout the text, you will find forms and tables you can customize by adding your contact information and printing them on your company letterhead.

3. Some chapters contain a *Supporting Scripts* section. Review the scripts to determine whether they fit how you do business. Practice the scripts you select out-loud until you have mastered them.

Some agents find writing out their scripts on cards is helpful. Others record their scripts and then listen to them while driving.

4. At the end of each of the first 14 chapters you will find an action plan that includes recommendations on how to implement the strategies covered in the chapter. Place a plus (**+**) next to each strategy you intend to implement.

5. When you begin to implement changes in your business, avoid trying to accomplish too much at one time. This can overwhelm you. Instead, experiment with one new strategy at a time. Determine what works best for you and *make those strategies a permanent part of your business.*

6. Reports from the Field provide additional strategies from agents who are on the front lines fighting the discount battle. As you read these reports, notice that the agents use only one or two strategies supported by some simple scripts to secure the listing. In addition, note their level of confidence. All of them believe they are worth the fee they charge. Clients are attracted to agents who believe they can get the job done.

7. Appendix A contains a list of tools and resources to support the concepts covered in this book.

The Outcome

By implementing the guidelines in this book, you will be able to:

1. Differentiate yourself and your services from the competition.

2. Motivate the seller to use your services because of the value you provide.

3. Dramatically reduce the probability you will have to defend your commission.

4. Be able to successfully defend your commission if necessary.

As in any type of war, lead with your strengths. Since most agents use traditional marketing, this is an excellent place to begin your battle plan.

Reports from the Field
Demand Your Self Worth!
Barb Van Stensel
Keller Williams Chicago

I believe that real estate agents that apply themselves in the industry, working it fully, deserve to be paid a professional salary. When I list a property, I pay myself according to the difficulty of the file. Since I'm usually the one to keep the file going and close it, I usually pay myself more than the buyer's agent.

If you ever find yourself becoming angry during a transaction, it may be because you are underpaid. Attorneys are paid according to their level of professionalism, training, skill, and the number of cases they win. Some doctors work in general medicine while others specialize in transplant programs. The level of pay depends upon the level of skill, knowledge and ability to be successful. The same should hold true for real estate professionals. That's why I charge differing fees for divorce cases and foreclosures. It takes a high level of concentration and energy to keep everyone focused. If the property is high-end, I look at the amount of time, uniqueness of the estate, and calculate my commission accordingly.

How can I charge my clients more money to close their file than an average agent? Because I'm worth it. Do I compete with other agents at times? Yes, I do. But if the seller doesn't understand my full value, then there may not be the connection and hence the file will be difficult. I would rather be paid what I am worth on files that require my skill than to sit at my desk and brew about how much of a jerk my client is, when in total reality, I was the jerk for taking the file below my income earning level!

If someone wants to discount, go ahead. Sure some of those files close but believe me, that seller wasn't represented to the fullest and usually pays in the end at the closing. My attitude about agents who discount is they don't believe in themselves enough and hence show it in their fee. Do I put down the other agents? No. If I did that, I would be discounting my self worth.

I recently had a file where the client was a buyer and tried selling their home three times but failed to do so. It should have raised a red flag with me when I represented them on the purchase of their new home because it was a nightmare. For example, they showed up 1.5 hours late for the closing and never apologized to anybody.

We all have choices in life. We must value ourselves more as real estate professionals and not as agents. We must realize that under-cutting each other is only selling ourselves short. Sellers should connect with us because of our personalities, skills, and the value we provide. We should be paid accordingly. If I do not connect with a seller, I don't take the listing. Why force yourself upon a seller, discount your commission, and lower your self worth just to beat the competition? Ultimately, it's about connection with the client. Undercutting each other only results in unhappiness, lower productivity, and a miserable career.

The choice is yours! Now go out and demand your self worth!

Chapter 2:
Start with Yourself:
Winning the Psychological War

Old habit of mind is one of the toughest things to get away from in the world. It transmits itself like physical form and feature.

— Mark Twain

What I do now and what I will add to my business:
Put a checkmark (√) next to what you do now. Leave the remaining items blank. Review the action steps at the end of the chapter to determine the strategies you will implement in your business.

____ 1. I establish strong personal connections with my clients.

____ 2. I am a master of the inventory.

____ 3. I present a strong, professional image.

____ 4. I can identify at least three ways I differ from most agents and can show my clients how these differences benefit them.

____ 5. I have at least two specific niches I service.

____ 6. Most people say I speak well. I avoid using slang, foul language, and am easy to understand.

Fighting the Internal Battle

The most important part of your Waging War Battle Plan will be the internal psychological war with yourself. Winning this war is a perpetual process. We are constantly under attack from both internal and external forces.

To win the psychological battle you must exude professionalism and confidence. Clients have radar much like people who date—they can tell when someone is desperate and they usually shy away from them. On the other hand, the individual who is confident, who does not need the business, and who has zero attachment to the decisions clients make, will consistently attract others.

The First Agent to Reach the Consumer Wins!

The 2004 National Association of Realtors® (NAR) Profile of Home Buyers and Sellers found 73 percent of all sellers only interviewed one agent prior to listing their home. Another 14 percent only interviewed two. This means 87 percent of the time you only have to overcome one competitor to obtain the listing. To win the psychological war, focus on becoming the first agent to talk to new leads.

Local Trumps Out of Area

While marketing and prospecting must reach local, national, and international clients, ultimately real estate is a local business. For buyers, the volume your firm sells makes little difference. In contrast, sellers normally list their property with one of the top three companies in their area. Large companies have more listings and this translates into more buyer leads. Consequently, when sellers decide to list their home, they normally seek out the agent and company doing the most business in their neighborhood. Buyers normally contact the agent or company with the most listings in the area where they would like to live.

Experience vs. Johnny-Come-Lately

Many discounters are Johnny-come-latelys who appear during strong sellers' markets. These companies lack the experience and credibility of traditional real estate firms. In fact, huge companies such as Sears, Merrill Lynch, and a number of banks have tried to cut into our business and ultimately fell by the wayside. Frankly, very few of today's discount firms will survive the next major market downturn.

Most full service agents cope with disclosure problems, title problems, and legal issues daily. In contrast, the Johnny-come-lately discounters lack a proven track record in assisting consumers with these very sticky and potentially litigious situations. At the time this book went to press,

Texas had just implemented a new regulation requiring all real estate brokers to provide a minimum amount of service. Discounters and on-line brokers now have to present and negotiate offers in addition to placing the property in the MLS. This new regulation greatly increases the probability the discounter or on-line brokerage will be subject to future litigation. This will drive up their operating costs, which in turn, can drive up how much they charge to sell a property.

Personal Connection is Still the Name of the Game

When past clients have trust and confidence in you, they are unlikely to do business with a stranger they met on the Internet. The most common error agents make is taking these precious personal relationships for granted. According to the 2004 NAR Buyer and Seller Profile, 82 percent of all sellers surveyed said they would use their real estate agent again. Only 31 percent of the sellers surveyed said they actually used the same agent. Agents often assume these wonderful people will remember to call them. Nothing could be further from the truth. Most people do what is expedient. Remember, 73 percent of all sellers do business with the first Realtor® they contact. Unless you have a strategy to prospect your database regularly, these precious leads may go to the agent who knocks on the sellers' door the morning they decide to list.

Knowledgeable and Professional

People draw conclusions about what kind of person you are within seconds of meeting you. The old adage, "You never have a second chance to make a good first impression" is true. People judge you based upon how you look and how you speak. Consequently, you only have seconds to make a favorable impression on potential clients. To appear knowledgeable and professional in person, follow these key steps:

1. *Master the inventory*

   One common trait all top producers share is excellent product knowledge. This is particularly true among people who sell estates. Clients want to know you can accurately price their property, aggressively market it, and successfully close the transaction once the property is under contract. For the areas where you work, you should be able to name the best-priced listings, how much it costs to purchase a typical three or four bedroom home, as well as what types of properties are available in various price ranges.

2. *Back to basics*

Everybody knows what is required to generate sales—you must generate leads and convert them into closed business. To do this, you need to master the basics of the business. What is the average market time in your area? Are you in a buyers', sellers', or flat market? Do you prospect for leads daily? What is your marketing plan? How do you protect the seller if the buyer does not perform? Without mastery of these fundamentals, your business will be hit or miss at best. Even worse, you will not exude the same confidence as the person who has taken the time and effort to become a master.

3. *Dress for success*

People make judgments based upon appearance. As a rule of thumb, dress the way your clientele dresses when they are at work. Spend the money to have at least two high quality outfits that you can mix and match (dark slacks, dark skirt, dark jacket, contrasting light jacket, sweater, shirt/blouse). Understated classics are generally better for business, especially since they never go out of style. Save your trendy clothing, jewelry, and piercings for when you are off work. Keep your clothes clean and your shoes polished. Run-down heels are the mark of someone who does not care about their appearance. People judge your attention to detail based upon a variety of factors. The first one they notice, however, is your appearance.

4. *What you say and how you say it*

You can look like a beggar, but if you speak beautifully, people will assume you are being shabby by choice. When you speak, slow down and speak clearly. Fast speech can make you appear like the stereotypical fast-talking salesperson. Avoid using slang, contractions, and chewing gum while at work. Also, avoid using foul language and never criticize anyone, especially your competitors. Religion and politics are also taboo. Finally, if you have a heavy accent or if you want to improve how you speak, consider taking a diction class or joining a group such as Toastmasters.

Psychological research shows like attracts like. Presenting a high quality image with high quality supporting business materials enhances the probability you will receive a full commission. In contrast, failing to value yourself increases the probability the seller will ask you to reduce your commission.

5. *What makes you unique?*

To brand your business, focus on what is unique about you and couple this with your function rather than your name. Advertisers bombard us daily with the names of people, products, and places. As a result, most people have a hard time remembering names. On the other hand, unusual names or names tied to a specific function tend to be easier to remember. Standing out from the competition requires you to capitalize on your unique qualities as well as unique services you provide. For example, if you are an avid golfer who specializes in resort properties, you could brand your business using any of the following:

HighlandHillsGolfHomes.com
*Hit a hole in one when you purchase
your next new home!*

JimAgentSellsLakeviewGolfHomes.com
*Live in a home where every day seems
like a vacation!*

Your marketing materials could show you sitting in a golf cart or teeing off with your For Sale sign nearby. In the two examples above, also note how the geographical location is linked with a specific benefit to the consumer.

6. *What's your niche?*

Almost all top producers have two or three specific niches they service. A niche can be a geographical farm or a specific market segment such as first time buyers or entrepreneurs who work from home. During the next five years, hot niches include Baby Boomers who are downsizing, immigrants, stay-at-home working moms, and people who speak languages other than English. If you are not niche marketing, becoming an expert in a specific area can reap huge rewards.

Reports from the Field

This Is Not a Chinese Restaurant

Gail Crann, Keller Williams Realty
Austin, Texas

When someone asks me to discount, I respond by saying, "No, and let me tell you why. In order to do that, I would have to offer a variety of products from which you can choose. This is not a Chinese restaurant where you pick an item from each column on the menu. I have only one product. The product I offer is a Mercedes Benz in terms of real estate service—it's not a Hyundai. If something less meets your needs, I'm not the right agent for you."

Depending upon the client, I sometimes use a different approach when they ask me to discount. For example, if the seller is a programmer with an excellent reputation, I'll ask her to imagine that she has received a job offer from another company. The new company thinks she is terrific and would like her to come to work for 33 percent less than she is earning currently. I then ask, "Would you take a job for 33 percent less than what you earn currently?" The answer is always "No." My response is, "Just like you, I could not fulfill your expectations of the highest quality service for less money."

People appreciate my directness. I am also highly accountable to my clients. When sellers pay a full commission, they expect and deserve accountability from their agent. My job is to accentuate the pluses and to minimize the minuses. Having a top-notch virtual tour is critical. When there are plenty of similar properties on the market, my role is to make my listings stand out. I hire a top-notch videographer to shoot their virtual tour, provide staging services, and make sure the sellers have the highest quality professional brochure.

Most agents tell the sellers what they will do. When you list the services you provide, the sellers keep a mental checklist and price each item. Often times they're thinking, "Well, it doesn't cost that much." Instead, I tell them what I don't do. "I don't take your listing and walk away. I don't walk away from problems. I don't pretend to be a jack-of-all-trades. I know who the best service providers are and I hold them accountable for doing the job right. I don't advertise in the local paper because last year it did not generate a single sale."

When someone tells me they're thinking about listing with a discounter, I tell them, "You're capable of doing this yourself. You care about your property, you would have to do the showings and open houses anyway, and you will probably have a better result."

Sometimes I'll meet sellers who are focused only on the commission. As soon as I realize this is the case, I tell them, "I'm not the right Realtor® for you. It's better for me to let you down now than it would be to disappoint you later."

Are We Our Own Worst Enemy?

What may be hurting us more than anything is our own attitude. According to Steve Murray, the Editor of *Real Trends:*

> "While nearly three-fourths of consumers were fairly satisfied with the use of associates, sales associates thought that only one-fourth of consumers would have rated them that high. In short, we are facing a crisis of confidence at the foundation level of our business...Yes, commission rates and splits are under pressure and have been for more than 10 years. But we also see great improvements in consumer satisfaction with "one-stop" shopping and the emergence of true "real estate service" companies, beyond realty firms. We are seeing a growing number of firms that want to use our listings as bait to capture customers, yet our share of all transactions in the hottest market in history remains steady. And the number of qualified leads coming directly from the Internet is as high from broker sites as it is from national sites. The brokerage industry has stolen the benefits of the Internet from those who would use it against us so far."

Steve Murray has it right. Full service brokerage continues to maintain a steady percentage of customers, despite the fact discounters, lead aggregators, and other big businesses are all trying to gain a piece of the pie. Ultimately, to win the psychological war, you must be prepared to win your own internal battle. If you sit back and do nothing, commissions will continue to decline and your business will continue to migrate to competitors who were better prepared for battle.

Chapter 2 Action Plan

To improve your professional image, use the suggestions below or re-write them so they fit the action that you would like to take. Place a plus (+) next to each item you plan to implement in your business. Leave the remaining items blank. Remember, trying to implement too much at one time can overwhelm you. If you select more than one item, place the items in priority order and work on implementing one item at a time. Once you implement the first item, move on to subsequent items.

Action Steps

_____ 1. I will build stronger connections with clients by listening more carefully.

_____ 2. To keep my client relationships strong, I will contact past clients at least six times per year either by mail, e-mail, or in person.

_____ 3. For the next thirty days, I will spend at least 15 minutes per day upgrading my knowledge of the inventory.

_____ 4. I will upgrade my professional image by improving my appearance.

_____ 5. I will upgrade the quality of my presentation materials.

_____ 6. During the next year, I will take at least two training classes to increase my real estate expertise.

_____ 7. I will identify three ways my services differ from those provided by other agents and write out at least one way these differences benefit my clients.

_____ 8. I will add at least one new niche to my business in the next 90 days.

_____ 9. I will focus on speaking more clearly.

____10. I will upgrade my speech by avoiding the use of slang and/or foul language.

Avoid the temptation to tell sellers how good you are. Instead, let them experience your professionalism firsthand.

How you present yourself involves more than your appearance or speech patterns. Equally important is how you relate to your clients and to other agents.

Chapter 3
Winning the Psychological War
Part 2: How to Avoid Shooting
Yourself in the Foot

*He will win who knows when to fight
and when not to fight.*

—Sun Tzu Wu

What I do now and what I will add to my business:
Put a checkmark (√) next to what you do now. Leave the remaining items blank. Review the action steps at the end of the chapter to determine the strategies you will implement in your business.

_____ 1. I avoid saying negative things about my competitors, even if they are true.

_____ 2. I avoid making statements that imply all agents charge six percent.

_____ 3. My listing consultation focuses on how my services help the sellers achieve the highest price possible rather than my personal achievements.

_____ 4. My marketing materials and my listing consultation are client-centric rather than agent-centric.

_____ 5. I use "you" language rather than "I" language during my seller and buyer consultations.

Don't Yield to Temptation

Sometimes agents are tempted to criticize their competitors. If you win the listing by bad-mouthing the competition, promising more than you can deliver, or making misleading statements, you may lose the war by ruining your own reputation. Remember, the path to winning is through personal excellence.

One of the quickest ways to shoot yourself in the foot is to violate Article 15 of the Realtor® Code of Ethics:

Realtors® shall not knowingly or recklessly make false or misleading statements about competitors, their businesses, or their business practices.

If you feel tempted to criticize a competitor's business practices, count to ten and bring the focus back to "What we do that makes us different." Remember, even in large metropolitan areas, the real estate community is small. Clients come and go, but the agents you work with will be around for years to come. Furthermore, when you make negative remarks about competitors, you are opening yourself up to disciplinary action by your Board of Realtors®, possible loss of your license, and, in some cases, potential litigation.

A second way to shoot yourself in the foot is to tell sellers "Everyone charges six percent" or "No one will show your home if you list for less than six percent." The federal government strictly enforces the antitrust compliance provisions for our industry. What this means is that neither associations nor their members collectively set the price of services provided by real estate professionals. Each firm sets its own policy in this area. According to National Association of Realtors®:

The firm's sales associates must take care to present pricing policies to prospective clients in a manner that is consistent with the fact that the fees or prices are independently established. This means they should never respond to a question about fees by suggesting that all competitors in the market follow the same pricing practices or to a policy of the local board or association of Realtors® that supposedly prohibits or discourages price competition.

Specifically, NEVER make statements like any of the following:

1. If you don't list at six percent, other agents will not show your property.

2. Agents don't show properties that do not have a full commission.

3. All agents who belong to our Board of Realtors® charge six percent.

4. If you list with a discount broker, other agents will refuse to show your property.

5. If you list with a discount broker, you will have fewer showings since agents show the listings with the highest commissions first.

Honest and Accurate

To win the consumer, honesty and accuracy are pivotal. If you misrepresent your services to the seller or fail to deliver what you promise, you lose the seller's trust. You also lose future referrals. If you deliberately misrepresent sales data, you can lose your license. There are so many ways win the consumer; there is no excuse to misrepresent your services or those of your competitors. Tell the truth, do what you say you will do, and walk away from situations where you are tempted to do otherwise.

Client-Centric Not Agent-Centric

Throughout the 1990s, trainers emphasized the importance of image marketing and sharing your accomplishments as the primary way to achieve credibility and win business. This led both agents and companies to focus on the "We're number one" approach. This approach misses two primary points. First, sellers and buyers have no interest in hearing how great we are. All they care about is the "WIIFM" principle—"What's in it for me?" More importantly, when we are talking about ourselves, we are not building our relationship with the seller. The stronger our connection is with our clients, the less likely they are to use another agent.

A quick way to check this in your consultations is to examine how often you use "I" language. When you say "I," the focus is on you. In contrast, when you use "you" language, you become client-centric. Throughout this book, you will notice most scripts utilize "you" language rather than "I" language.

Many agents have worked hard to earn professional designations from the National Association of Realtors®. Agents who earn these designations often offer a higher standard of service. Sadly, a large portion of the buying public has no idea what "GRI" or "CRB" means or how it will affect the sale of their property. If you are going to use a designation during your listing consultation, demonstrate how your designation assists the sellers in achieving their goals. Remember, your clients only care about what's in it for them.

The best way to approach both buyers and sellers is to be client-centric rather than agent-centric. The shift is simple, yet the results are profound. When you discuss the services you provide, do so in the context of how those services assist the seller in obtaining the highest price possible in the shortest time. When you focus on how your services benefit the client, the probability of obtaining the listing at a full commission increases dramatically.

If You're Playing Defense, You're Losing

The moment you go into defense mode, you have lost the battle. A recent training session illustrated this point quite well. During the session, I asked the 50 agents in the room to give me their best strategies for overcoming the commission objection. Here is the summary of what they said:

Strategy 1:
Explain how the commission is split four ways and that you only receive 1.5 percent, not the entire 6 percent. The balance of the commission goes to your broker, to the other agent, and to that agent's broker.

Challenges with Strategy 1
Telling the seller you receive one-fourth of the commission puts you on the defense. The moment you begin justifying your commission, you are negotiating from weakness rather than strength. For example, during the role-play using this response, the agent playing the seller responded by saying, "Your broker is worth millions—tell him to take less." Now the agent has to defend the broker's commission as well.

A better response is to focus on the seller's real question—"What's in it for me?" What the seller really wants to know is how they can obtain the most money possible for their property. Instead of telling the seller what happens with the commission, turn the tables to your advantage by asking the following question:

Is it correct to say that your real concern is how to get the highest price possible for your property?

The obvious answer is, "Yes."

To achieve highest price possible, you will need to do three things: first, you must have maximum exposure to the buyers in the marketplace by positioning your property competitively in terms of price. Second, since most properties sell through a broker, you must do everything possible to make your property attractive to buyers' agents. Third, you will need an agent who can negotiate the highest possible price for your property. So let's look at how you can obtain the highest price possible for your property.

At this point, you will discuss the specific strategies you will use to help the seller achieve the highest price possible for their property.

Strategy 2
Tell the seller about the services you provide so they can see the value of paying a full commission.

Challenges with Strategy 2
This is a great strategy, provided you are not telling the seller how great you and your company are. Rather than defending by telling, use a question instead. For example,

Here is a list of the services we provide at different commission rates. Which of these options best suits your needs?

The beauty of this approach is most sellers want full service. Rather than defending your commission, simply ask the sellers to make a choice. Given the choice between full service (800 call capture technology, pay-per-click Internet marketing, print advertising, 360 tour, open houses) and less than full service (limited ads, no 360 tour, no open houses), most people will choose the full service route.

Strategy 3:
Tell the seller that the buyers' agents show the properties with the highest commissions first.

Challenges with Strategy 3

If you use this approach, a shrewd seller may say, "We'll pay the selling agent three percent—you take two percent." Even more dangerous, however, is the potential accusation of price-fixing. Again, NAR prohibits Realtors® from using any suggestion of price fixing. A better approach would be to use the following script:

> *To obtain the highest price possible for your property, you need someone who is a powerful negotiator—isn't that correct?*

The obvious answer is "Yes."

> *So if you hire an agent who can't even negotiate a full commission on their own behalf, how effective do you think they will be in negotiating the maximum price for your property?*

Notice in each example, the shift is from telling to asking a question. The moment you start telling rather than asking, you lose the battle. Instead, ask questions with the idea of staying focused on the Seller's real concern—"What's in it for me?"

To unlock the door to a full commission during your next listing consultation, remember to stay focused on how the seller can obtain the highest price possible for their property in the shortest time.

Chapter 3 Action Plan

Excellent relationships with both clients and other agents are pivotal to having a successful real estate career. If you are not a client-centric agent, now is an excellent time to make the shift by implementing the action steps below. When you compete against other agents, never do so by criticizing what they do. Instead, state your value, share the market statistics, and allow your clients to make their own decisions. Your role is to show the sellers how your services help them obtain the highest price possible for their property.

As in Chapter 2, you can use the suggestions below or rewrite them so they fit the action you would like to take. Place a plus (+) next to each item you plan to implement in your business. Leave the remaining items blank. If you elect to implement more than one item, place them in priority order. Once you implement the first item, move on to subsequent items.

Action Steps

_____ 1. I will avoid saying negative things about my competitors.

_____ 2. During my listing consultation, I will avoid making statements that imply all agents charge six percent.

_____ 3. During my next listing consultation, I will focus on how my services help the sellers achieve the highest price possible for their property.

_____ 4. I will change my marketing materials and my listing consultation so they are client-centric rather than agent-centric.

_____ 5. I will shift to using "you" language rather than using "I" language during my seller and buyer consultations.

Since many agents still use an agent-centric approach, making the shift to being client-centric can give you a major competitive advantage.

Plan Your Waging War
Marketing Campaign

The language of marketing has been borrowed from the military. (We "launch" a marketing "campaign.") We talk and act like generals; we just don't think and plan like generals. It's time to apply the principles of military strategy to our marketing operations and thus increase the chances of success.
                              —Ries and Trout, *Marketing Warfare*

Chapter 4
Winning the Agent Campaign

If everyone is thinking alike, then
somebody isn't thinking.
—General George Patton

What I do now and what I will add to my business:

Put a checkmark (√) next to what you do now. Leave the remaining items blank. Review the action steps at the end of the chapter to determine the strategies you will implement in your business.

____ 1. My current listing consultation incorporates all of the "Four P's." (*Pound* a sign in the front yard, *Put* the property in the MLS, *Place* an ad in the paper, and *Post* pictures to the web.)

____ 2. When I list a property, I market it to other agents who also have listings in the same area.

____ 3. I market my listings to agents with listings in move-up areas.

____ 4. I market my listings to agents who hold open house in areas that are priced approximately 20 to 30 percent higher than the property I am marketing.

The next ten chapters outline four primary fronts where you conduct your Waging War Marketing Campaign:

1. The Agent Campaign
2. The Public Campaign
3. The Web Campaign
4. The Customer Service Campaign

Most agents market to the public and spend little time conducting an agent campaign. Consequently, marketing to other agents can be an excellent way to obtain a strategic advantage. Before delving into how to market more effectively to this group, remember this important point:

Your goal is to provide three to five services your competitors lack. In most cases, this is all you will need to win the customer and the campaign.

Wage War Unconventionally

How you elect to wage your personal marketing campaign depends upon your personality, motivation, and effectiveness using various marketing options. No matter how you choose to wage your personal marketing war, however, your primary objective is to persuade the consumer to do business with you rather than with someone else. Instead of focusing on what most agents do, the following chapters examine innovative twists few competitors utilize.

Most agents wage war using the "Four P" approach to marketing. Notice there is a fifth "P" on the list below to represent what really happens:

1. Pound a sign in the front yard
2. Put the property in the MLS
3. Place an ad in the paper
4. Post the pictures to the web
5. Pray it will sell

Many traditional, on-line, and discount competitors provide sellers with exactly the same services. The question you must answer is, "What services do you offer sellers over and beyond what your competitors provide?"

Agents know they should market to other agents, yet the large majority spend their marketing dollars on marketing to the public. Sellers believe newspaper and web advertising is critical, yet most homes sell through other agents. Since very few agents emphasize how they will market to other agents during their listing consultation, explaining this process is an easy way to differentiate yourself from your competitors.

Hit the Bull's-eye by Marketing to Allies

Effectively marketing your listings to other agents involves much more than placing a property in the MLS. To differentiate yourself from your competitors, incorporate any of the three strategies below:

1. *Market to agents who have listings in the same area*
   Agents who have a listing in the same area are usually generating buyer leads from their advertising. Capitalize on this by contacting them personally to provide information about your listing. If you have posted a virtual tour to your website, contact the other agents and ask if they would like to receive the link so they can preview the property from the convenience of their own computer.

2. *Market to agents who have listings in move-up neighborhoods*
   Unless your listing is a starter home, most communities have one or two move-up or feeder areas. Many of these owners would like to purchase something larger and/or nicer in the same area. Personally contact each listing agent since these sellers may soon be buyers.

3. *Market to agents who hold open houses on more expensive properties in the same area*
   Typically, open house buyers look at homes priced 20 to 30 percent higher than they can afford. Staying in touch with listing agents who represent higher priced properties near your listing can often generate a sale.

Ultimately, your goal is to reach as many potential buyers as possible. Marketing to other agents is an excellent place to begin.

Chapter 4 Supporting Scripts

By target marketing agents who are most likely to have buyers for the seller's property, you increase the probability the seller will obtain a higher price in a shorter time. The script below will help you incorporate the strategies from this chapter in your listing consultation:

In order to obtain the highest price possible for your property, you must have maximum exposure to the brokerage community. To do this, I will actively market your listing to the other agents in your area by holding broker open houses, sending them an on-line color brochure, and contacting other listing and buyer agents who may have buyers for your property. Is marketing to the brokerage community a service you want?

If "Yes," you have probably obtained the listing.

If "No," follow up by saying:

If I understand you correctly, you are not interested in marketing your property to the brokerage community. Did I get that right?

If they answer, "Yes," chances are high they will not list with you. You can explore further if you like, but in most cases, it's probably wise to leave. Before departing, let them know you are a full service broker and would be happy to work with them if they decide they want full service. Also, don't forget to thank the sellers for their time.

Once you complete your action steps for Chapter 4, go to Chapter 5 to learn about innovative strategies for marketing to the public.

Chapter 4 Action Plan

Take a hard look at your current listing consultation. What is your strategy for marketing your current listings? Do you offer all 'Four P's'? What else do you provide that distinguishes your services from competitors'? More importantly, did you describe these services to your sellers during your last listing consultation? Did you explain how you will market to other agents who have listings in the area or how you will target market buyers?

If you want to do a better job on your next listing consultation, determine which of the following action steps you would like to take to improve your business. Place a plus (+) next to each item you plan to implement in your business. Leave the remaining items blank. If you elect to implement more than one item, place them in priority order. Once you implement the first item, move on to subsequent items.

Action Steps

____ 1. I will incorporate all of the "Four P's" (*Pound* a sign in the front yard, *Put* the property in the MLS, *Place* an ad in the paper, and *Post* pictures to the web) in my listing consultation.

____ 2. When I list a property, I will market it to other agents who also have listings in the same area.

____ 3. I will market my listings to agents who have listings in move-up areas.

____ 4. I will market my listings to agents who hold open house in areas that are priced approximately 20 to 30 percent higher than the property I am marketing.

Taking the action steps above will strengthen your marketing to other agents. The next step is to conduct an effective public marketing campaign.

Chapter 5
Basic Weapons to Win the Public Campaign

Never interrupt your enemy when
he is making a mistake.
—Napoleon Bonaparte

What I do now and what I will add to my business:

Put a checkmark (√) next to what you do now. Leave the remaining items blank. Review the action steps at the end of the chapter to determine the strategies you will implement in your business.

_____ 1. Any mailing I do is followed up with face-to-face contact.

_____ 2. My marketing materials are client-centric, not agent-centric.

_____ 3. I spend the bulk of my marketing budget on marketing to people I know rather than marketing to strangers.

_____ 4. I regularly write handwritten notes to keep in contact with my referral database.

_____ 5. All of my mailing pieces have a call to action or some other benefit that motivates recipients to call me.

_____ 6. I target market my mailing pieces to specific niches or areas.

_____ 7. I regularly invite neighbors to my open houses.

_____ 8. I call other agents and invite them to attend my broker open houses.

_____ 9. I conduct 24-7 open houses with virtual tours on my website.

___10. I conduct invite-a-friend open houses.

___11. I use a CD brochure to market my listings.

___12. I invite sellers to assist me in creating the marketing program for their property.

___13. I invite buyers who view my listings to complete a showing survey.

Search for the Perfect Buyer

How can you reach the perfect buyer for your listing? If we had a crystal ball, we could select the one strategy that really works. Without the ability to foresee where the buyer will come from, however, we must capitalize on the gaps in our opponents' defenses and turn those into our own competitive advantage. The best way to capitalize on our enemies' vulnerabilities is to hit them with weapons they do not have in their arsenals. This chapter explores some innovative twists on several tried and true lead generation techniques.

Basic Weapon #1: The United States Mail

Do you market your services by mailing to a geographical farm or to a specific market niche such as developers or attorneys? Do you create a targeted marketing mailing program for each of your listings? To create the maximum return for your marketing dollar, you may need to revisit how you currently conduct your mailing campaigns.

Mailing alone is not enough
Unless you follow up with a telephone call or with some other type of personal communication, marketing by mail is passive. In general, it takes 18 to 36 months to build a successful geographical farm by mailing. You can speed up the process by door knocking, but it takes time to build people's trust. If you elect to mail without personally following up on your mailing pieces, there is a high probability you are wasting your money. The bottom line is people connect when they are face-to-face, not with a mailing piece.

Client-focused, not agent-focused
A common trap for many agents is sending out self-promotion pieces. Postcards or letters that feature information about the agent rather than useful information for the recipient do little to build connection. In contrast, a client-centered focus promotes connection. Remember, your recipient only cares about "What's in it for me?"

Market smarter
To maximize the results from your mailing budget, send out one hundred mailers to people you know five times per year rather than a single mailer to five hundred strangers. Besides asking for a referral, provide your recipients with something they value, such as coupons, school schedules, fire safety information, etc. Marketing to strengthen personal connection yields the greatest return on your investment.

A simple, powerful connection builder
An often-neglected connection builder is the hand-written note. When someone visits your open house, sends you a referral, or when you must reconnect with a past client, writing a quick note has a powerful impact. Since few competitors utilize this powerful tool, hand-written notes are an excellent way to distinguish yourself from your competition.

Your mailing must have a purpose beyond "getting your name out there"
Mailing is an excellent way to expand your database. Unfortunately, if your sole purpose is to publicize your services, you will seldom have a great result. Instead, offer coupons from local vendors, a complimentary telephone evaluation of the recipient's property value, or useful information about homeownership. Another smart strategy is to use a tear-off stamped postcard the recipient can use to contact you.

To send or not to send
Few agents question why full service real estate companies send Just Listed or Just Sold cards for them. Companies mail these cards for agents because it promotes the company's brand. Because advertisers constantly bombard us with names of people, products, and businesses, most people have a hard time remembering names. People

are also more likely to remember a name they have seen repeatedly. The result is Just Listed or Just Sold cards reinforce the brokerage name rather than the agent's name. If you are going to mail Just Listed or Just Sold cards, give the people who receive the card a reason to contact you. Motivate the recipient to take action by inviting them to enter a drawing or by offering them a money-saving report. If your broker provides this service for you, by all means, take advantage of it. If not, spend your marketing dollars where they will yield a better return.

Use a laser, not a shotgun
Effective marketing targets a specific audience. Most mega-producers service two or three specific niches. They also target specific types of buyers for their listings. In contrast, less productive agents often use a shotgun approach that lacks a specific focus. To enhance your marketing efforts, narrow your focus by asking, "Who is the ideal buyer is for the listing?" "Where does this person live currently?" "How can I best reach this person?" To achieve this goal, carefully evaluate who will be the best candidates to purchase your listings. Familiarize yourself with area demographics. Identify the move-up areas that feed sales where the listing is located and design your marketing plan to reach those buyers. For example, if you are marketing a first-time buyer property, the most likely purchasers are high-end renters who live in the same area. If you are marketing a more expensive property, the "move-up area" will be properties priced at 20 to 30 percent less than your listing. Design your marketing plan with laser precision to reach these buyers, share your plan as part of your listing consultation, and watch the discount objection melt away.

If you're going to market by mail, be smart about how you do it—focus on building connection, market to the specific needs of specific groups, and keep track of what works. Most importantly, ASK FOR THE ORDER! If you fail to ask for the order on every single item you mail, you are wasting your money no matter what you send.

Basic Weapon #2: Open House
Should you hold open houses? There is no correct answer to this question. Thousands of top producers have built their businesses by holding

open house. Just as many never hold an open house unless it is for other agents to preview the property.

Open house is worthwhile provided you use the open house as a prospecting opportunity, can convert open house visitors into leads, and routinely follow up with leads generated. Unfortunately, few agents conduct effective open houses. In fact, NAR reports that 98 percent of all agents fail to follow up on all open house leads. If you do follow up on open house leads, you are outperforming 98 percent of the competition.

Since most discounters require the owner to hold their own open houses, an agent-hosted open house provides several benefits. First, agents usually are more effective at converting open house leads into signed business. An agent can delve into a buyer's finances where the seller may not be comfortable in doing so. Agents normally prescreen buyers prior to taking them out to look at property. Sellers who host their own opens have no way of knowing if their open house visitors are legitimate buyers or if they are criminals looking for an easy mark.

If you have more than two listings, managing your open house schedule can be challenging. Since you cannot personally hold more than two listings open on a Sunday, you will need to other alternatives. One strategy is to hold opens on other days of the week, especially weekdays during the summer. Many agents use "twilight opens" to catch potential buyers on their way home from work. You can also stagger your open house times or conduct a "progressive open house" where a number of agents in the same area hold their listings open on the same day.

Four Powerful Open House Strategies

Since most discounters do not provide these services, the four open house strategies below are powerful weapons in overcoming the discount objection.

Strategy 1: Open house with hand-delivered invitations
This strategy effectively combats discounters who require sellers to conduct their own open houses. It is also an excellent strategy for generating listing leads. To use this approach, print out attractive invitations and deliver them to the neighbors as well as residents of move-up areas. The invitation should come from the seller rather than from you.

Research shows Saturday morning is generally the best time to deliver the invitations. When you knock on a prospect's door, use the following script:

Mr. and Mrs. Jones have just listed their property at 123 Main Street and have asked me to personally invite you to our open house on Saturday from 1:00-4:00 PM. We will be serving refreshments. Will you be able to attend?

To generate good names from the open, hold a drawing for a gift certificate or movie tickets. You will be amazed at how easily you can generate leads.

Strategy 2: Broker's opens

Sellers almost never hold broker's open house. The 2004 NAR Profile of Home Buyers and Sellers showed 78 percent of all properties sell through cooperating brokers. Maximum exposure to the brokerage community is critical if the seller hopes to achieve the highest possible price. To attract more agents to your broker open houses, try serving food.

An even better approach is to hold a progressive open house. Contact other agents who have listings in the area and arrange for each agent to host a different course. Offer appetizers at the first houses, main courses in the middle, and desserts at the final house. If you feed them, they will come. To drive attendance, hold a drawing for a gift basket or for lottery tickets. To qualify, visitors must sign in at each house on the progressive.

A smart way to create even more traffic at your broker opens is to call other agents and invite them to attend. Use the following script:

Mr. and Mrs. Jones have asked me to personally invite you to our broker's open house brunch on Tuesday from 10:00 AM to noon at 123 Main Street. Will you be able to attend?

If you are doing a progressive open, you can drive traffic by advertising it in your local paper or with brochures delivered to the brokers in the area.

Strategy 3: 24-7 open house

Hold a 24-7 open house on your website by posting a virtual tour PLUS at least 15 to 25 digital photos of the property. If you have several listings, you can create your own virtual open house tour. Sellers like the idea that buyers can preview their home on-line rather than in person. Use your print advertising to drive people to your 24-7 open houses. Run an ad like the one below:

Preview twelve properties in the Shaker Heights area from the convenience of your own computer with ABC Realty's 24-7 Open House. We're open for business right now! Drop by and see us at: ShakerHeightsOpenNow.com

Strategy 4: Invite-a-friend open house

Another excellent way to distinguish your services from those of discounters is to hold an "invite-a-friend" open house. This open house is exclusively for the seller's friends and acquaintances. The seller puts together the guest list, selects a date, and you handle the other details. The invitations ask the seller's guests to invite a friend who may be interested in purchasing the property. This approach is a fun way to generate both buyer and seller leads.

Basic Weapon #3: Customization Increases Connection

Most agents provide brochures for their listings, yet few customize their marketing materials in a way that involves the seller in the process. To distinguish yourself from the competition, use the customization strategies below.

CD virtual tour

Many agents create virtual tours for their listings. To distinguish yourself from competitors, make CD copies of the virtual tour that include your name, your contact information, and the property address. If you do not have a virtual tour, take at least 15 to 20 digital pictures of the property and save them to a CD. Make the CDs available to all agents who show the property as well as to any open house visitors. Instead of having the brochure delivered to other agents, send the CD. You can also send the CDs to relocation buyers as well as using them when you door knock. You can customize the look of your CDs by having labels printed with your name, phone number, and website address.

Increase connection by seeking the seller's input
Forming a strong connection with the seller may be your best line of defense against competitors. To increase your connection with the sellers, ask for their input on how to market their property. Allow the sellers to select the postcards, ads, and brochures they would like you to use. While some sellers have little attachment to what you do, most respond very favorably to this approach.

Allowing the seller to have input into your marketing campaign strengthens your personal connection. It is also a critical part of a "presumptive close." (Presumptive close refers to acting as if you have obtained the listing.) When the seller starts selecting their marketing materials, you probably have the listing. Better yet, few discounters can compete since they do not offer this level of service.

Basic Weapon #4: Post-Showing Follow-up

The best agents consistently follow up on every showing. An even better approach, however, is to solicit feedback directly from buyers after each showing. There are three ways to do this. The first option is to call the buyer's agent after the showing. This is difficult because you must track down the buyer's agent and then hope the agent remembers the buyer's response. You could also send an e-mail, except 58 percent of all agents do not respond to e-mail inquiries of any type. The best strategy is to use the half-page survey below. Staple the survey to the property brochure and ask the buyer to complete the survey before leaving. For an example, see Table 1.

Table 1
SHOWING SURVEY

1. Is this property one you would consider buying?
   _____Yes   _____ No

2. Compared to other properties you have seen, the price of this property is:
   _____ Low _____ About right _____ High

3. Compared to other properties you have seen, the condition of this property is:
   _____ Not as good
   _____ About the same
   _____ Better

4. What did you like the most about this property?

   _____

   _____

5. What did you like the least about this property?

   _____

   _____

Thank You for Sharing Your Feedback!
Sally Agent, ABC Realty
1-800-555-1212

Chapter 5 Supporting Scripts

Basic Weapon #1: United States Mail

Targeted mailings maximize the property's exposure to high-probability buyers. To implement this strategy during your next listing consultation, use the following script.

> ### Script #1: Targeted marketing
> *In order to obtain the highest price possible for your property, it is important to reach the buyers who are most likely to purchase your property. In most cases, your ideal buyer will come through someone who lives in your neighborhood or lives in a less expensive neighborhood nearby. This targeted marketing approach will help you sell your home more quickly. Is targeted marketing a service you want?*

Basic Weapon #2: Open House

Most agents only hold traditional open house. Using all four types of open house dramatically increases the property's exposure to both the public and the brokerage community. Use the script below to add this strategy to your next listing consultation. (If you elect to use only two or three types of open house rather than all four, alter the script accordingly.)

> ### Script #2: Open House
> *In addition to holding the usual Sunday open house, many agents also hold a broker's open house where they invite other brokers to preview the property. Did you know there are two other important ways to market your property using open house?*

Wait for their reply and then continue:

> *The third way to obtain maximum exposure to the marketplace is by holding a 24-7 open house on my website. To do this, we will need a virtual tour and at least ten digital pictures of your property. Is having a 24-7 open house a service you want?*

If the sellers say, "Yes," you can discuss setting up the virtual tour and taking photos. This also means you probably have the listing. If the sellers say, "No," or if you want to offer an additional service, continue with the script below:

> *A fourth way to obtain maximum exposure to the marketplace is by holding an "Invite-a-friend" open house. This is a private open house for your personal guest list. I will host the open and handle all the details. The invitations will encourage your guests to "invite a friend." Even if their friends are not interested, they may know someone who is. Is holding an invite-a-friend open house a service you want?*

Again, if the sellers agree to have an invite-a-friend open, you have just secured the listing.

Basic Weapon #3: Customization Increases Connection

Creating a customized marketing plan during your listing consultation is an excellent way to build connection with the seller. Most sellers are also interested in seeing how you will market their property. Asking sellers which marketing services they would like to use is a way to do a presumptive close. With each item they select, you increase the probability of obtaining the listing at a full commission.

Script #3: Customized marketing plan
In order to obtain the highest price possible for your property, you will need a customized marketing plan that makes your property stand out from the crowd. One strategy for doing this is to post at least ten digital pictures and a virtual tour of your property on Realtor.com. A second strategy is to use a CD brochure plus a paper brochure. The CD brochure allows buyers to view your property without having to disturb you. Is having a CD brochure plus multiple pictures and a virtual tour on Realtor.com a service you want?

Basic Weapon #4: Post-showing Follow-up

Immediate feedback allows the agent and the sellers to identify obstacles that may be blocking the sale. This shortens market time while increasing the likelihood that the sellers will obtain a higher price. If you plan to use a showing survey with your listings, use the script below to describe it during your listing consultation.

Script #4: Showing Survey
Each time an agent shows your property, we will ask the buyers to complete this showing survey.

(Hand the sellers the survey.)

If you are not receiving offers, this strategy will help you spot what is preventing the sale. Is having feedback from buyers a service you want?

The more services you provide, the more likely you are to obtain a full commission. In addition, the showing survey is a powerful tool when you need a price reduction. If buyers consistently point out that the price is too high, it's much harder for the sellers to deny that they are overpriced.

Chapter 5 Action Plan

If you already prospect by mailing or holding open house, the basic weapons outlined above are simple to implement. Rather than marketing to strangers, consider reallocating your marketing budget so you spend more money marketing to people you know. The same is true of open house. Door knocking to invite neighbors to your open house generates a consistent flow of traffic. It also generates new listings and more income.

While many agents generate leads, a large proportion do not consistently follow up on those leads. This is especially true for open house leads where only two percent of all agents follow up. Thus, you can easily differentiate yourself from competitors simply be engaging in consistent lead follow-up.

As in previous chapters, place a plus (+) next to the items you would like to add to your business. If the items below do not fit what you would like to do, rewrite them so they do. Once you finish, place the items you checked in priority order. Again, avoid trying to change too much at once. Baby steps over time create huge results.

Action Steps

____ 1. When I mail out a marketing piece, I will follow up with face-to-face contact.

____ 2. My future marketing pieces will be client-centric, not agent-centric.

____ 3. I will reallocate my marketing budget so the bulk of it is spent on marketing to people I know rather than marketing to strangers.

____ 4. I will write at least ten handwritten notes each week to keep in contact with my referral database.

____ 5. My future mailing pieces will contain a call to action or some other benefit that motivates recipients to call me.

____ 6. I will target my future mailing pieces to specific niches or areas.

____ 7. I will invite neighbors to attend my future open houses.

____ 8. Prior to holding a broker's open house, I will call other agents and invite them to attend.

____ 9. For each of my listings, I will hold a 24-7 open house by posting a virtual tour and at least ten digital pictures of the property on my website.

____10. I will include an invite-a-friend open house as one of the services I provide to sellers during my listing consultation.

____11. As part of my marketing campaign, I will create a CD brochure to market my listings.

____12. During my listing consultation, I will invite sellers to assist me in creating the marketing program for their property.

____13. I will invite buyers who view my listings to complete a showing survey.

As in previous chapters, determine which action steps you will take to improve your traditional marketing efforts. Place them in priority order and implement them one at a time. Once you have identified your action steps from this chapter, go to Chapter 6 to learn about a key weapon you will need for your Waging War Listing consultation.

Chapter 6
The Public Campaign:
Seize the Golden Moment of Opportunity

To improve the golden moment of opportunity, and catch
the good that is within our reach, is the great art of life.
—Samuel Johnson

What I do now and what I will add to my business:

Put a checkmark (√) next to what you do now. Leave the remaining items blank. Review the action steps at the end of the chapter to determine the strategies you will implement in your business.

____ 1. I currently have an "800 Call Capture" (IVR) system.

____ 2. I use my Call Capture system to track the effectiveness of my marketing campaigns.

____ 3. I regularly demonstrate how my Call Capture system works during my listing consultations.

Capture More Listings with Call Capture

Of all the weapons available to capture the business from your competitors, 800 Call Capture (IVR or Interactive Voice Recognition) often yields the most decisive victory. According to the 2004 NAR Profile of Home Buyers and Sellers, 73 percent of all sellers work with the first agent with whom they make contact. Another 14 percent only speak with two agents before they list. Consequently, 73 percent of the time all you need to do to win the listing is to be the first agent to speak with the seller. If you implement only one strategy from this book, obtain an 800 Call Capture System.

Eliminate Opponents with a Knock-Out Blow

The most powerful tool in your listing arsenal is the telephone. Surprisingly, few agents use telephone technology effectively, especially during their listing consultation. If you are not using a Call Capture technology, you are missing one of the most compelling tools available to defend your commission.

Call Capture technology is an excellent way to provide potential leads with what they want, when they want it. The typical Call Capture System relies on an 800 number tied to a specific numerical code for each of your listings. When a caller dials your 800 number plus the code from an ad or a sign, the caller hears a detailed description of the property. Because you paid for the 800 call, the telephone company gives you access to the caller's phone number and address. Even if the caller has blocked their number with Caller ID or if they are calling from an unlisted number, the fact they called your 800 number entitles you to this information.

The best Call Capture systems send the caller's contact information to you immediately via your cell phone, text messaging, fax, or e-mail. This means you have access to leads when their interest is the greatest—the moment they picked up the phone to listen to your pre-recorded message. Remember what the NAR study revealed:

Seventy-three percent of the sellers did business with the first agent with whom they made contact.

Furthermore, people often call after hours or on weekends when the agents are unavailable. When a lead cannot locate the information they want, they call the next phone number on their list. The person who makes the first contact usually captures the sale.

An 800 Call Capture System is a powerful tool to overcome resistance people may have about contacting an agent. Most people who call on an ad or a sign want information on the property and want to hang up as quickly as possible. Because they believe they will not have to speak with an agent, leads are more likely to call a pre-recorded message. Since your message is available 24-7, leads can call at their convenience. In addition, people are much more likely to call an 800 number, especially if they live outside the area.

What you may find surprising is the quality of leads generated. Gary Elwood of Proquest Technologies shared a study his company did with

200 hundred agents who use their 800 Call Capture service. The survey followed up on 25,000 leads to determine what percentage had listed or sold a piece of real estate in the last 60 days. The answer was a surprising 33 percent. This is the same conversion rate most agents experience with referrals and is 16 times higher than the one to two percent conversion rate from cold calling or door knocking. Moreover, of those who did not purchase in the preceding 60 days, an additional one-third had very clear buying criteria. What this means is that over 50 percent of these leads are A or B+ leads, that is, "right now" business; people who intend to sell or buy in the next 60 days.

Elwood's study revealed another important finding: adding a toll-free Call Capture number to your print advertising or to your Just Listed and Just Sold cards dramatically improves the effectiveness of these campaigns. For example, the agent who places an ad in their local *Homes Magazine* usually generates 5 to 15 calls from a typical ad. By adding the "free information hotline," the number of calls typically increases to over 75.

Another advantage of this technology is that you can provide a separate identification number for each of your listings and ads. The system tracks how many calls each number receives. This in turn allows you to track which ads are effective and which ads you will need to revise or eliminate. As a result, you can trim advertising expenditures by spending money only in areas that yield the greatest results.

Call Capture Enhances Your Other Campaigns

Very few agents track the effectiveness of their advertising in the newspaper, in a homes magazine, or in other advertising media. Consequently, they have no idea which ads drive people to respond and which ads do nothing. A Call Capture system, however, lets you show the seller how many responses you receive from each ad you place. This allows you to target your advertising where you have the greatest response. For example, some sellers believe print advertising works as an effective tool to sell their home. If you run a $50 ad that no one calls on, your Call Capture system will document this approach does not work. You can alter the ad, but if you still receive no calls, spend your money elsewhere. Your Call Capture system provides the solid ammunition you need to help the seller understand where and when marketing works.

In terms of demonstrating this as a benefit to the seller, being able to quickly spot where and when advertising works is critical to achieving the highest price possible for the property. Running an ineffective ad week after week lengthens market time and costs the seller money.

If your competitor reconnaissance reveals your opponents do not have Call Capture technology, this is the first item you should reference during your Waging War listing consultation. If your opponents do have Call Capture, you may need a more aggressive technique to overcome the enemy.

Chapter 6 Supporting Scripts

Call Capture provides you with numerous advantages. A key issue is immediacy. Because the system pages you immediately after your caller hangs up, you can call back the lead when their interest is the greatest.

This is an important weapon to use during listing appointments. To illustrate how this technology benefits the seller, have the seller call the telephone number on any of the mailing pieces they received from competitors. In most cases, the floor broker will answer and botch the call. Then turn on your cell phone and have them call your 800 number. When your cell phone rings, show them the phone number. This one simple tool can often wipe out competitors in a single, deadly stroke.

Call Capture technology also allows you to control the leads you generate. This alone is worth the investment in the technology. Most agents place their company's phone number on their mailings since they do not have a Call Capture system. If this is the case, guess who receives most of the calls your advertising generates—the floor broker. In contrast, Call Capture ensures that your leads always reach you. If you would like to implement Call Capture in your listing consultation, use either of the two following scripts.

Script #1:
Many companies advertise your property on the web and in the newspaper. Did you know in most offices that 90 percent of all those leads are lost since the person answering the phone fails to obtain the caller's number?

(Wait for a response)

To obtain the highest price possible for your property, your real estate agent must capture every potential lead. My 800 Call Capture system obtains accurate contact data over 90 percent of the time. Before you list your property, call my 800 number and then call my competitors to see who does the best job in obtaining your phone number. Does this strategy work for you?

Script #2:

To obtain the highest price possible for your property, it is important for your agent to obtain accurate contact data from every lead their advertising generates, wouldn't you agree?

Wait for their response and continue:

Did you know that most offices fail to convert 90 percent of the ad and sign calls they receive? This means 90 percent of the leads that call on the other company's listings will be lost. Would you like to see how my 800 Call Capture technology accurately captures the names and phone numbers of over 90 percent of the people who call on our ads and yard signs?

Demonstrate the system and then close by saying:

By capturing the call when the buyer's interest is the greatest, you increase the probability the buyer will purchase your property rather than someone else's. Is Call Capture a service you want?*

*Additional Call Capture Scripts are in Chapter 18.

Chapter 6 Action Plan

If you elect to take only one action step from reading this book, obtain an 800 Call Capture system. Because most offices still rely on agents to answer telephone inquiries, 90 percent of their telephone leads are lost. In contrast, your system will capture close to 100 percent of the phone inquiries on your ads, signs, and website.

During your listing consultation, the first service you should demonstrate that differentiates you from competitors is your Call Capture system. To obtain more listings at a full commission, make the three action steps below your highest priority. Place a plus (+) beside each step you will take and rewrite any of the items if necessary.

Action Steps

____ 1. I will set up an 800 Call Capture system within the next seven days.*

____ 2. Before each listing appointment, I will record a special message for the sellers to hear as part of my listing consultation.

____ 3. During my listing consultation, I will show the sellers the benefits of working with my Call Capture system.

*See "Resources" in Appendix A for additional information.

Call Capture is a powerful marketing tool. Another powerful marketing tool few agents use is cable television advertising.

Chapter 7
The Public Campaign:
Aim Your Remote Control at a
Full Commission

This isn't brain surgery; it's just television.
—David Letterman

What I do now and what I will add to my business:
Put a checkmark (√) next to what you do now. Leave the remaining items blank. Review the action steps at the end of the chapter to determine the strategies you will implement in your business.

_____ 1. I advertise on cable television.

_____ 2. I target my cable television advertising to specific niches or market areas.

_____ 3. My cable television advertising uses a memorable name that makes it easy for viewers to contact me.

Outflank Discounters with Cable Television Advertising

If you want to be the victor who earns full commissions, the route to victory may be as near as your remote control.

Virtually all agents rely on print advertising to market their listings. Today's big push is to market using the web. The problem with both print and web advertising, however, is they seldom target a specific market. Cable television provides a tremendous strategic advantage that allows you to outflank your competitors.

Before embarking on a cable television advertising campaign, consider the following benefits. Due to the proliferation of cable and satellite television, cable television advertising costs have declined dramatically. Local cable operators actively seek local advertisers as an additional revenue source. When the cable operator lacks local advertising, they run national ads to fill space. The local cable company receives no revenue from running these ads. Thus, local cable television operators are eager to do business with agents because agent advertising represents more revenue for them. In fact, 30- to 60-second ads can be as little as $6 to $12 per spot. Furthermore, cable television allows you to target specific geographical areas at a minimal cost. Compared to classified advertising costs, cable television is a real bargain.

Learn from the Big Guns

To create an effective cable television ad campaign, observe how major companies target their products to different audiences. The folks on Madison Avenue know what works: targeted advertising aimed at specific niches creates the greatest return on their advertising dollars. For example, auto manufacturers carefully target their television advertising campaigns to fit the demographics they want to reach. You are more likely to find a BMW or Jaguar commercial on a political show such as *Meet the Press*. If you are watching *American Idol*, however, you are much more likely to see a commercial for a cute convertible, a muscle car, or a great looking truck costing half the price of the luxury car. No matter what you watch, the commercials reveal the audience demographics.

Thus, begin your cable television campaign by targeting a specific geographical market. Cable television allows you to target your audience by zip code, county, and/or region. You can also target your audience using a geographical center point and then going out two to five miles from that central point.

Where and How to Advertise

To refine your target marketing, determine what types of clients normally do business with you. Begin by examining the listings and sales you have made over the last two years and aim your marketing at the audience you normally attract. Are your clients up and coming young professionals, boomers, or retirees? Where do they live? Next, determine your top three targets in terms of geographical region, income, and property type (i.e., single family, condominium, resort, golf course, military, investment, etc.). To obtain the greatest return on your advertising dollar, you must also know who buys your product as well as what television shows they watch. To make this determination, use the following guidelines.

1. If you have a geographical farm, make this a primary target. Due to the "Do Not Call" list, agents often have to rely on door knocking or direct mail. Cable television offers an entirely different approach for reaching your geographical farm. Typically, it takes six "impressions" (i.e., the number of times a person sees your name) before a prospect will consider contacting you. The repetition of your name, along with the other approaches we will discuss, greatly increases the probability a seller will contact you. The next question is what are the people in your farm watching? Your local cable service can provide answers since they price their advertising based upon viewing patterns. For example, if you want to reach stay-at-home moms, advertise on stations running large numbers of baby commercials.

2. If you're selling foreclosures, fixer-uppers, or investment properties, consider advertising on stock market shows, remodeling shows such as *This Old House* and *Trading Spaces,* or interior decorating shows. A good way to identify where to advertise is to watch where Home Depot and Lowe's advertise. If either of these companies advertises on a program, you can be sure the show reaches homeowners.

3. If you are selling resort or golf course property, consider advertising on the travel channels or on sports stations that televise golf tournaments. Again, watch where big companies are advertising and match your advertising to fit the demographics suggested by your observations.

4. If you sell estates, watch for advertisements for expensive cars, "Platinum" credit cards, and expensive hotels. The travel channels may also be a good choice. You can rest assured that if there is a Mercedes, Jaguar, or BMW commercial, the audience watching the show has the money to afford the product.

Remember, major companies spend millions analyzing how to target their audience accurately. Take advantage of this free research. Better yet, consider hiring a Public Relations specialist who can help you with many of the strategies outlined below.

Crafting Your Advertising Strategy

The next strategy to address is advertising. Do you want to advertise your listings by using a virtual tour? Do you want to focus on marketing your brand? Is your goal to drive people to your website? The strategy you choose will influence the type of ad you will run. Each approach has pros and cons.

Advertising Specific Properties

Electing to advertise specific listings is a great way to generate listing leads. Sellers love having their property advertised on television. Depending upon the size of your market, you could put together a weekly or monthly cable television program showcasing your listings. To minimize costs, you could also do this with other agents from your office.

The challenge with this approach, however, is the time required to produce the program each week. A simple way to do this is to have a virtual tour for each one of your properties. When you take a listing, you record your comments about the property as part of the virtual tour. Your television program then becomes a series of virtual tours.

If you expect people to call from your ad, having a Call Capture system is a necessity. If your goal is to drive people to your website, you must have a strategy for harvesting names. This can include free reports, registering for a drawing, or offering web visitors a free membership in your Homeowner's Club.

Promoting Your Personal Brand

Promote your personal brand with a series of offers that drive visitors to your website or encourage them to call your 800 Call Capture number. This strategy allows you to produce two or three commercials that run consistently. Remember, in advertising, repeated product exposure is the name of the game. For example, advertisers often repeat the same commercial twice within a two-minute period. First, the station runs a

30-second commercial spot from the first advertiser. Next, they run a second ad. The station then reruns the first ad. People immediately notice the commercial was a repeat. Even though it is aggravating, the repetition increases the viewer's product recognition. While repetition is crucial, it is probably unwise to aggravate your viewing audience.

The downside of advertising your brand is sellers will be more excited about your television campaign if it includes their home. Nevertheless, even if you do not advertise specific properties, cable television is still a huge asset. Use your cable television advertising to drive people to your website where they can view a comprehensive virtual tour of your listings.

Creating a Simple Television Ad

In terms of your ads, you will need a 30-second commercial and a 60-second commercial. Depending upon available space, the cable company will decide which ad it will run. A professionally produced 30- or 60-second spot can cost $5,000 to $10,000. Clearly, this is much more than most agents are willing to spend. If you want to produce your own ad, however, here are some ways to do it.

1. Usually, the least expensive approach is to have a single screen with a voice-over. Adding virtual tours or advertising specific listings significantly increases production costs. By keeping it simple, you control costs and deliver a consistent message.

2. Prominently display your easy-to-recall website name. Since people are poor at remembering names, select a website address that references function. For example:

   > AustinProbateSellers.com
   > LakesideHorseProperties.com
   > SanDiegoOceanViewHomes.com

   You can use your name and picture, but you will waste your advertising dollars if you fail to use a function rather than just your name.

3. Include your 800 Call Capture number. This allows people to choose whether they want to contact you by phone or on the web.

4. To gather names from your ad, motivate the viewer to visit your website. Do this by offering money-saving reports (i.e., "Save Thousands on Your Next Purchase"), drawings, or by offering a complimentary Competitive Market Analysis (CMA).

5. Hire a professional graphic designer to achieve a high quality, professional look. A good design will range in price from $250 to $700.

6. Write a 30- and a 60-second message. Most people speak approximately 150 to 160 words per minute. Thus, your 30-second spot will be approximately 75 to 85 words and your 60-second spot will be about 150 to 170 words. In terms of what to say, listen to the ads placed by the national real estate companies. Your script should reference the visuals on your screen—your website address, your phone number, and your offer of free services such as a complimentary telephone evaluation of their property's value, money-saving coupons, or virtual tours on your website.

7. Record your commercial in a sound studio using a professional sound engineer. This will result in a higher quality product. For example, some people "pop" their "P's" when they record. The sound engineer sets up a "P-popper" to block this sound from the mike. The sound engineer can also remove the sound of you taking a breath. Heavy breathing is certainly not the image you want to convey to your viewing audience. If your area does not have a professional recording studio, check with your local community college or local radio station for suggestions. Also, if you do not have a great voice, hire someone who does.

Placing Your Commercial

The next question is how to reach your targeted audience. Cable television lets you advertise by zip code or by a given radius from a central location.

In terms of the cost, cable advertisers usually sell "blocks" of users. (A typical block might be 79,000 users.) You can also advertise by county, state, or region. Depending on the size of your viewing area, you could be advertising on *CNN, Discovery,* or *ESPN* for as little as $8 to $10 per spot.

Television Creates Instant Credibility
Lee Konowe, Marketing Director
Northern Virginia Fine Homes
Reston, Virginia

Our company is based just outside Washington, D.C., where there is a substantial amount of discounting. My wife and business partner, Denese Konowe, has been advertising on cable television with great success. We use the pre-canned commercials from www.E-Agent.biz and advertise to three very distinct audiences. Aaron Brown's 10:00 PM news broadcast on *CNN* draws a clique audience that enjoys in-depth news analysis. We match our marketing message to the audience demographic, which is sophisticated and highly intellectual. The second demographic that we target are viewers of the *Larry King Show*. This show reaches a general audience and we tailor our message to have a wide appeal. The third demographic we target is the *Mansion Programs* on the *Home and Garden Channel*. This advertising specifically targets the luxury home market.

Advertising on cable television gives you instant credibility. Clients seldom ask Denese to reduce her commission. The clients who contact us believe they are getting such a high level, celebrated agent that it would be tawdry to ask for a discount.

In addition to cable television advertising, we also provide a "talking house" service, virtual tour, plus a host of other Internet tools. Moreover, we refuse to do both sides of the same transaction. We hold brokers' opens and aggressively market our listings on the net. Denese also makes a point of being available to her clients almost any time they need her. When a seller signs up with us, they have the sole and exclusive use of all of our resources.

As part of our listing presentation, we review the average number of days our listings stay on the market as compared to other firms. We also compare the seller's net after commissions. In both cases, our statistics show we sell properties quicker, for more money, and with fewer cancelled transactions. In the rare case where someone does ask us to discount, we point out this is our fee structure and it is not negotiable. If the services are *extra* ordinary, then the person is making the decision whether to purchase the full array of services we provide. The bottom line is, these are our services and this is what we charge.

Chapter 7 Supporting Scripts

Cable television advertising can target the areas where the most potential buyers for the seller's property live. It can be particularly effective if you live in a cold climate or serve a market area that is sparsely populated. Using advertising demographics allows you to target specific niche markets such as first time homebuyers, resort properties, or estates. In addition, buyers are more likely to contact a broker whose name they recognize. To implement cable television in your listing consultation, use the script below:

Have you seen any of our cable television ads?

Wait for their response and then continue:

Advertising on cable television allows us to attract more buyers for our listings. Our goal is to drive more traffic to our website to view the digital pictures and the virtual tour we will make of your property. More traffic means more exposure for your property. Is maximum exposure for your property a service you want?

Chapter 7 Action Plan

Take a hard look at your current advertising budget. Are you receiving an adequate return on your mailings? If not, cable television may be an excellent alternative for increasing your name recognition and for generating leads. Because few agents use this approach, it can be an important way to differentiate yourself from your competitors.

To implement cable television advertising in your business, follow the steps below. You will find additional resources in Appendix A. Place a plus (+) next to each item you plan to implement in your business.

Action Steps

____ 1. I will contact a local cable television company to determine the feasibility of implementing a cable television advertising campaign in my market area.

____ 2. I will contact a local broadcasting professional to obtain an estimate for producing a 30-second and a 60-second cable television ad.

____ 3. I will create a marketing budget for my cable television advertising campaign and compare it to what I do currently. If the numbers make sense, I will produce the ads.

____ 4. My cable television advertising will use a memorable name and a clear value proposition that makes it easy for listeners to contact me.

____ 5. Once the ads are produced, I will target my cable television advertising to specific niches or market areas.

____ 6. I will post my television ads to my own website.

____ 7. At the end of 90 days, I will compare the number of leads I obtain from cable television advertising to determine whether it is worth the continued investment.

Cable television is a great way to advertise. If you need more ammunition or if television isn't right for you, there's another excellent alternative. Because people now spend more time than ever commuting, radio advertising is an excellent way to differentiate your services from those provided by competitors.

Chapter 8
The Public Campaign:
Capture Rush Hour Business

Advertising is what you do when you
can't go see somebody. That's all it is.
—Fairfax Cone

What I do now and what I will add to my business:

Put a checkmark (√) next to what you do now. Leave the remaining items blank. Review the action steps at the end of the chapter to determine the strategies you will implement in your business.

___ 1. I advertise on the radio.

___ 2. I target my radio advertising to specific niches or market areas.

___ 3. My contact information and my value proposition are easy for listeners to remember.

___ 4. I host my own real estate radio show.

Be the First Agent to Capture Rush Hour Business

If you have a great voice, radio may be the perfect vehicle to capture all those potential clients trapped in rush hour traffic. Like local cable television, local radio stations depend upon their listening community for commercials. In terms of where to advertise, the same principles apply. The first issue to consider is the type of programming and the target market you would like to reach. For example, jazz and classical stations are more likely to have affluent listeners than hip-hop or rap stations. Talk radio typically draws a more educated, older audience. Higher education usually equates with higher income. Other excellent choices include any type of show dealing with investments, gardening, or home improvement.

To evaluate where to advertise, listen to the commercials. As with cable television, if major home supply warehouses are advertising on a particular station, you can be sure a large number of homeowners are listening to that station. The same is true if you hear commercials for mortgage lending, high-end automobiles, or business credit cards. Again, it pays to take advantage of this free market research.

Selecting a Format

There are two primary options for radio advertising. The first is to run a standard 30- or 60-second ad. The second is to have your own show.

1. *Creating a radio commercial*

    As with cable television, you will need a 30- and a 60-second spot. Remember, a 30-second spot will be approximately 75 to 85 words and your 60-second spot will be about 150 to 170 words.

    The challenge with radio advertising is creating a commercial that drives home your name and phone number. Consequently, your branding, your website URL (web address), and your telephone number are critical. Follow the same guidelines discussed in the preceding chapter. Rather than using your name to brand your business, use what you do, whom you do it with, and where you do it. You should also follow the same format for your website address.

    Since most listeners will be unable to write down your information, you must repeat your web address and telephone number at least three times. This also means your phone number and web address must be easy to remember. People usually can recall repeated number sequences or a name that can be used instead of a phone number. For example:

    1-800-Atlanta
    1-800-4buyers
    1-800-200-1234

    Since you must repeat your contact information three times, you must have an intriguing message that motivates the listener to contact you. The key point to remember is the message must be about the *listener's* needs rather than about how great you are. Here are some examples:

Thinking about buying or selling a home? If so, visit us at www.Bloomfieldhomes.com to see all the current listings on our local Multiple Listing Service. At Bloomfieldhomes.com learn how to save thousands on your next sale or purchase. If you are already a homeowner, Bloomfieldhomes.com is pleased to provide money-saving coupons from local Bloomfield merchants. Visit our website today at BloomfieldHomes.com or call us at 888-200-1234—that's 888-200-1234.

Need to sell your home fast?
Let AustinSellerServices.com show you how to reach buyers worldwide with our ten-point international marketing plan. Get the highest price possible in the shortest time with AustinSellerServices.com's exclusive web placement plan that markets your property through five different real estate websites plus most major search engines. Our free money-saving reports and E-coupons can save you thousands of dollars whether you are selling, buying, or just enjoying being a homeowner. Remember, when you need to buy or sell, AustinSellerServices.com is the best way for you to obtain the best price possible. Visit our website today or call us at 1-800-Austin4U. Again, that's 1-800-Austin, the number 4, and the letter U—1-800 Austin4U when you need to buy or sell Austin real estate.

In each of the two commercials above, notice there is no mention of the agent's name. Instead, the commercial references the website URL. Ideally, your goal is to drive people to your website or to your Call Capture system where you can harvest their contact information.

Other items you can include are drawings, information on foreclosure properties, probates, first-time buyers, etc. The goal is to evaluate the listening audience and tailor your commercials to fit their needs.

As in all types of advertising, repetition is critical. Name recognition builds up over time. Change your offers periodically, but always remember to reference your contact information at least three times.

2. *Creating Your Own Radio Show*

Creating a radio show can be a fun and exciting challenge that reaps huge rewards. Begin the process by searching for a radio station that has space for your show. This is easier in small towns than it is in large cities. Contact local stations to determine the feasibility of hosting your own show. Normally they will require an audition tape. To succeed, you will need a clear, distinct voice that is easy to listen to and easy to understand. You will also have to be able to think on your feet since most radio is live.

When things go wrong, and they always do, you must remain calm while coping with the problem. Before you launch into doing live broadcasts, it would be wise to practice by recording yourself and having the tapes evaluated by a broadcast professional.

Focus on the needs of your audience rather than doing an infomercial for you. Use the commercial spots to plug your services, but keep the show focused on the listener's needs. Throughout the show, invite listeners to visit your website to obtain E-coupons from local merchants or to enter your weekly drawing for movie tickets or a dinner.

In terms of what to include, interest rate updates are critical. You can also discuss the impact of new legislation on homeownership. If you live in a small city, you may elect to update your listeners on upcoming local events. Make your show more interesting by inviting guests who can discuss a variety of real estate related topics. Use a question and answer format. For example, invite a foreclosure specialist to discuss how to find and purchase foreclosure properties. Lenders make great guests since they can address different types of mortgages as well as the wisdom of purchasing vs. refinancing and remodeling. Decorators and landscapers are excellent resources for helping owners to spruce up their homes.

No matter whom you invite, it would be wise to tape them ahead of time to hear how they handle themselves in a question and answer format. Avoid guests who have poor speaking voices, poor grammar, or who are unable to give clear, concise answers to your questions.

Chapter 8 Supporting Scripts

Like cable television advertising, radio advertising builds name recognition while helping you reach specific niche markets. Targeted advertising to high-probability purchasers increases the likelihood of a fast sale and a higher purchase price for the seller. If you elect to use radio advertising as part of your listing consultation, use the script below:

Have you heard any of our radio commercials?

Wait for their response and then continue:

Radio advertising allows us to attract more buyers for our listings. We target our ads based upon listening patterns so we can attract high probability buyers for our listings. The ads direct listeners to our website where they can view the digital pictures and the virtual tour we will make of your property. More traffic means more exposure for your property. Is maximum exposure for your property a service you want?

Chapter 8 Action Plan

Compared to cable television advertising, radio advertising is much less expensive to produce. A major difference, however, is that radio employs more of a shotgun approach. It is virtually impossible to target specific geographical niches. On the other hand, you can target special interest groups such as sports fans, travel enthusiasts, first time homebuyers, investors, etc. As suggested in Chapter 7, examine your current advertising budget to determine whether you are receiving an adequate return on your advertising dollars. If not, diverting some of your marketing budget into radio advertising may be a wise decision. Again, since very few agents advertise on the radio, it can be an important way to differentiate yourself from your competitors.

To implement radio advertising into your business, follow the steps below. You will find additional resources in Appendix A. Place a plus (+) next to each item you plan to implement in your business. If you select more than one action step, place them in priority order. Rewrite any action steps that need alteration.

Action Steps

_____ 1. I will investigate the feasibility of implementing a radio advertising campaign by contacting at least two local radio stations to determine the rates, guidelines, and demographics of their listening audiences.

_____ 2. I will contact a local broadcasting professional to help me determine whether I should do my own commercials or hire talent to do them for me.

_____ 3. I will obtain an estimate for producing a 30-second and a 60-second radio ad.

_____ 4. I will create a marketing budget for my radio advertising campaign and compare it to what I do currently. If the numbers make sense, I will produce the ads.

____ 5. My radio ads will use a memorable name and a clear value proposition that makes it easy for listeners to contact me.

____ 6. Once the ads are finished, I will target special interest groups that fit the demographics of where I do business.

____ 7. I will post my radio ads to my own website.

____ 8. At the end of 90 days, I will compare the number of leads I obtain from radio advertising to determine whether it is worth the continued investment.

____ 9. If my radio advertising is successful, I will investigate the feasibility of doing my own real estate radio show.

Radio and television advertising are powerful ways to build your business that few agents use. No one, however, can afford to ignore the importance of having a powerful website.

Chapter 9
Winning the Web Campaign:
Kill the Competition with a Killer Website

In war there is no substitute for victory.
—General Douglas MacArthur

What I do now and what I will add to my business:
Put a checkmark (√) next to what you do now. Leave the remaining items blank. Review the action steps at the end of the chapter to determine the strategies you will implement in your business.

____ 1. I have a client-centric web site.

____ 2. My website is easy to navigate, provides visitors with what they want, and allows visitors to "opt in."

____ 3. My website accesses the MLS through IDX (Internet Data Exchange) or VOW (Virtual Office Website).

____ 4. My website has a "call to action" that motivates the web visitor to provide their personal contact information.

____ 5. My web address is easy to remember and references function rather than my name.

____ 6. I respond to all web inquiries on the same day they are received.

____ 7. I have my 800 Call Capture number on my website.

____ 8. I host a neighborhood website for my local community.

Defend Your Commission with a Killer Website

If you want a first rate defense against both discounters and full service competitors, you need a killer personal website. Rather than using your website as an electronic business card, make it into a powerful lead conversion tool by following the guidelines below.

Client-Centric—Not Agent-Centric

Agents waste millions of advertising dollars making their websites about *them* rather than the web visitor. Advertising works best when it identifies a consumer need and then provides a solution to fulfill the need. Sadly, most agents believe being agent-centric is the key to attracting clients. Virtually all agents use their home page to post their picture and provide an infomercial about their accomplishments. To demonstrate this point, consider the information below that typifies many agent-centric websites:

> *Sally Agent is a residential real estate specialist who brings an impressive real estate and accounting background to her position. She believes clear communication with her clients is critical. Sally is enthusiastic, energetic, and has a strong desire to provide her clients with superior service. Her perseverance in solving problems allows her to achieve high levels of success in placing properties under contract and closing them. A native of Los Angeles, Sally has a BA from UCLA. She is a CPA, which provides her with a critical edge in today's highly competitive real estate field. She was "Rookie of the Year" and continues to receive awards for top production in Southern California.*

This information is all about the agent. There is no emphasis on the potential clients or their needs. This agent-centric approach relies on the false belief that clients choose their agent based upon the agent's achievements. Worse yet, there is no request to have the potential client call the agent for an appointment. Experience tells us virtually all clients select their agents based on two factors: personal connection and WIIFM—"What's in it for me?"

Now compare a different approach:

Selling or buying a home can be an intimidating process. How much is the property actually worth? What types of inspections are necessary? What are the current mortgage rates and how will they affect your ability to sell or buy? For the answers or to learn more about what is happening in the Los Angeles real estate market, click on any of the following icons:

- ◆ *Properties Currently Listed for Sale*
- ◆ *Comparable Sales Information*
- ◆ *How to Find the Best Mortgage Rates*
- ◆ *Advice for First Time Buyers*
- ◆ *Tax Tips for Home Buyers*
- ◆ *Living in L.A.—Schools, Transportation, Recreation, Shopping, and More*
- ◆ *Chamber of Commerce Information*
- ◆ *Tips for Home Safety*
- ◆ *Resources for Home Improvement*
- ◆ *Resources for Home Inspections*
- ◆ *Relocation Information*

If you would like to know what your property is worth or if you have questions about buying or selling, call Sally Agent today at 800-555-1212 for a personal consultation.

This client-centric approach has a number of distinct advantages over the agent-centric approach.

1. Using your website to pose questions and answer them in a detailed, professional fashion is an excellent strategy for demonstrating your expertise rather than just telling potential clients "I'm the expert."

2. When you provide comparable sales information as well as current inventory, you greatly increase the probability the client will contact you. If your current web page does not let you open

either your company's listings or those of your MLS without leaving your site, contact your web designer to learn how you can have web visitors open other sites without leaving your site.

3. Providing one-stop shopping by including Chamber of Commerce information, answers about buying and selling, mortgage information, etc., greatly reduces the probability potential clients will visit other websites since your site contains all the information they need.

4. The phrase, "Call Sally Agent today" is an embedded command to contact Sally about listing or buying a house. The potential client will be more likely to call an agent who has already provided them with value as compared to someone who has not.

5. Having an 800 number is smart for two reasons. First, potential clients, especially those who are relocating, are more likely to call you because the call is free. Second, your phone bill or your 800 Call Capture system will list the number from which they called. Thus, even if you miss their call, you can still follow up later.

Website Necessities

Before you purchase a website, make sure it meets the criteria below. If you already have a website and it lacks these features, contact your web company or web designer about upgrading.

1. *Easy navigation*
    When visitors reach your website, it should be easy to navigate as well as being user-friendly. "Navigation" refers to how easy it is to move from place to place on the site. "User friendly" refers to how quickly and easily your visitor can find what they are searching for on the web. Ask a friend who is not Internet-savvy to locate information on your website while you look over their shoulder. If your friend has difficulty, you need to revamp your site so it is easier to use.

2. *Give them what they want*

   According to an extensive research from Z57.com, web visitors only click on three things when they visit agent websites: "buyers" "sellers" and "find a property." To market proactively, you must focus on these three critical areas. There is nothing wrong with including other key phrases for the search engines, but make sure these three areas are prominently displayed on your site.

3. *Be the resource for neighborhood sales data*

   Visitors want to know how much properties are selling for in their area. If your Board of Realtors® allows you to post closed sales to the web, update all the sales for your service area at least once per month. If your Board does not permit posting of addresses and exact sales prices, you can post price ranges and general amenities. For example,

   $125,000-$150,000 Shady Hollow Subdivision
   3-bedroom 2.5 bath, pool, family room, 1 story, wooded lot

   4-bedroom 3.5 bath, family room, remodeled, 2 story brick traditional

   For additional information, e-mail us at (and insert your e-mail address)

4. *"Opt-in" is a necessity*

   With the changes in the spam laws, you must offer an "opt-in" feature for any communications you send from your site. "Opt-in" means the visitor voluntarily signs up to receive communications from you. It also means the individual may "opt-out" at any time. In addition to obeying the law, the advantage of using this approach is you are now using permission marketing. People are more receptive to your marketing efforts when they have made a conscious decision to request what you are sending.

5. *Quality matters*

   When it comes to web leads, quality is important. Like any other lead, you must qualify how good the lead actually is. For example, someone who requests all your reports on how to save money on a mortgage or regularly checks your site for MLS information is probably a serious purchaser. You can also qualify leads by asking them to complete specific information about what they are searching for or by asking to complete an on-line survey about their interests. You can then market to them based upon what they want, rather than what you think they want.

6. *Increase your stickiness*

   "Stickiness" refers to how long visitors stay on your site. To have visitors stay on your site longer, have a wide variety of resources visitors may find useful. For example, include a page of "Frequently Asked First-time Buyer Questions," a mortgage calculator, as well as Chamber of Commerce information for the areas you service. Other ways to increase stickiness include providing information on schools, crime statistics, transportation, recreation, etc.

7. *Change your site frequently*

   Give your visitors reasons to visit your site often. Since mortgage information changes constantly, you may want to provide a link to a lender who publishes today's mortgage rates. Another alternative is to sign up for a daily real estate news feed like the one provided by *Inman News* (www.Inman.com). Fresh information invites your visitor to return to your site repeatedly. Furthermore, the more professional your content appears, the more likely you are to hear from website visitors.

8. *Don't forget to ask for the order!*

   Make sure your website asks for the order on every page of your site. The most important place to do this is before and after each listing on your site.

   For a private showing or for additional information on this property, please e-mail me (insert your e-mail address) or call me (insert your phone number or pager number).

OR, for potential sellers:

Please click here (provide a link to your personal e-mail) for a no obligation telephone market analysis of your property.

OR,

Call me for more information on selling your home.

IDX or VOW: A Must-Have Weapon Discounters Can and Will Use Against You

The primary reason people visit your website is to preview properties. According to the 2004 NAR Profile of Home Buyers and Sellers, 93 percent of the web visitors said the primary thing they were looking for on-line was properties for sale. The same study also found the two most important features buyers look for in a real estate website are photos (84 percent) and property information (84 percent). Since you only have a few seconds to grab the visitor's attention before they surf to another site, providing what the web visitor wants is critical. If your website does not access a large number of listings and photos, there is little reason for the visitor to contact you.

To address this issue, provide a link on your site that accesses all of your company listings. Alternatively, you can jointly market your listings with several other agents from your company. The best solution, however, is to link to your local MLS using either IDX (Internet Data Exchange) or VOW (Virtual Office Website).

Probably the most contentious debate in our industry has been whether MLS systems should make secret MLS information available to people who are not licensed. For over 50 years, real estate professionals have used access to MLS information as a primary means to attract business. With the advent of Realtor.com, IDX, and VOWs, MLS information is no longer the driving force that attracts clients. Instead, what really matters to clients is something a website can never provide—wisdom and personal connection. You can only provide this through face-to-face contact. Remember, MLS data is the vehicle to begin building a personal connection with your web visitor.

Create a Call to Action

In addition to a VOW or IDX solution, effective web marketing also requires you to market actively rather than passively. Unless you take specific steps to make your web marketing efforts active, most visitors will have little motivation to contact you. The best website providers have a series of built-in devices allowing you to harvest the web visitor's contact information. You can use any of the five strategies below. Please note that in each example, the visitor has a choice of opting-in to receive future information. When you force people to provide information against their will, you will be unlikely to attract them as customers. Remember, demonstrating how your website motivates web visitors to contact you provides a powerful advantage over the competition.

Strategy 1: Provide E-coupons for local companies

Most businesses are eager to gain new customers. Coupons from local vendors are a great way to bring business to the door. Give visitors a choice of several different coupons and then have the visitor click on the coupon they want. Before the visitor prints the E-coupon, ask if the visitor would like to receive other money-saving coupons in the future. If so, have the visitor complete a form that includes their e-mail address and tells you what type of coupons they would like to receive. You can now permission-market legally to this web visitor. Not only does this strategy allow you to obtain good contact information from web visitors, it also provides a great reason to prospect local business owners.

Strategy 2: Provide an on-line course

While many agent websites offer free reports to attract web visitors, the lead you develop is a lead for a free report, not necessarily a buyer or a seller. A better strategy is to divide your free report into five to seven stand-alone units. Each stand-alone unit becomes part of an on-line course such as "Buying Your First Home" or "Maximizing the Profit from the Sale of Your Home." Your web visitors click on the link and provide their e-mail address to receive the free on-line course. This allows you to permission-market to the web visitor with something they want. Use an autoresponder system to send the first report immediately. Send subsequent units every three to five days.

Strategy 3: Offer a no-obligation Competitive Market Analysis (CMA) by telephone.

Agents have successfully used free CMAs for years as a way to attract business. Anyone who provides a valid property address is a solid lead. Normally the agent makes an appointment to drop off the CMA information in person. In many cases, however, the web visitor does not want an agent coming out to their home. They want to know about their property value, but are reluctant to have an agent pressuring them when they may not be ready to sell. Using a no-obligation CMA by telephone circumvents this problem. Once the seller gives you a property address and valid phone number, you can place them in a six- to ten-week postcard program to stay in touch. If the seller still hasn't listed after receiving six to ten contacts, call them back to offer them a quarterly update on prices.

Strategy 4: Become a VIP member

Everyone likes to feel important. You can offer special services to your VIP members, such as your Annual Report, invitations to your client appreciation events, etc. To join the VIP club, the only requirement is to have at least one other person register for your newsletter or other service.

Strategy 5: Provide a complimentary e-mail newsletter

Most people are curious about what sells in their neighborhood at what price. Many agent newsletters provide information about preparing your home for sale, interest rates, and other issues that are relevant only if you are buying or selling. Ninety-five percent of the people you contact are not in the market right now. Consequently, provide them with recent sales data plus general information related to issues of home ownership. For example, are there any changes in federal, state, or local laws that may affect improvements the owner would make to their property? Has the local school board raised the tax rate? Make what you send relevant to people who are enjoying their homes as well as those who may be listing or selling.

Reports from the Field
When You Pay Peanuts, You Get Monkeys
Malcolm Kaufman, McGuire Real Estate
San Francisco, California

When it comes to real estate, I'm a businessman first and foremost. I did acquisitions for ITT, was Vice President of Finance for Sega Enterprises, and was the founder/CEO of three different companies prior to starting my real estate career.

Real estate is a business, yet few clients view the purchase of their home as a business transaction. For most people, it is the largest financial transaction they will ever conduct. When I meet with client, I show them how property values have increased over the last fifteen years. I also review the other financial trends that can affect their sale or purchase so they have a complete picture of the current market conditions. For example, San Francisco has a very stringent rent control ordinance. Buyers and sellers must know how the rent control provisions affect their ability to occupy and enjoy their property.

In addition to evaluating the financial aspects of a sale, I also look at lifestyle decisions. For example, many homes in San Francisco have over 30 steps up to the front door. This can be an issue for people who are experiencing knee or hip problems or may be prone to them because of their age. It's important that sellers and buyers consider lifestyle factors that affect their sale or purchase, not just the price or the commission. Because I track all of these factors, I know the pulse of the San Francisco market better than anyone. Clients hire me first for my business expertise and second for my real estate experience.

What differentiates me from other agents? One unarguable difference is my *Pulse of the Market*© newsletter. This is linked to my website and is a major source of referrals. Each month I update my 2,500 readers on what is happening in a specific segment of the San Francisco market. My readers often share it with friends or relatives who are considering buying or selling. The *Pulse of the Market*© newsletter provides the best market intelligence possible to each of my clients. Basic Marketing 101 says, "Stay in front of your target market with something of value on a frequent basis."

When sellers ask me to discount my commission, I look them in the eye and tell them, "My policy is six percent. When you hire me, you're hiring the best. Since I'm a master at setting up the competitive environment among buyers, listing with me is the best way to obtain the highest amount for your property." I also stress that half the listing commission goes to the buyer's agent; we want to collectively incentivize those agents by providing the most competitive commission rate possible. Sellers never think of this.

If the sellers are adamant about discounting and it makes sense to take a reduction to obtain the listing, I will offer to reduce the commission to 5 3/4 percent. With me, it can be a long, slow process to go from six percent to five percent. I do not understand why agents immediately reduce commissions in 17-percent increments.

There's a saying in the Venture Capital community in Silicon Valley that "When you pay peanuts, you get monkeys." The bottom line is when clients focus only on the commission, they may get peanuts rather than dollars.

A Great Website is Easy to Find
and Easy to Remember

Since the public is constantly bombarded with product names, place names, company names, and people's names, using your name as part of your website address (URL) may make it hard for people to find you on the web. To make your web address memorable and easy to locate, it should incorporate the following:

1. The geographical area where you work

2. A term that references real estate such as "homes," "properties," "condominiums," "estates," etc.

3. The specific niche you service

For example, if your niche is selling lake properties in Austin, you might brand your site, AustinLakeProperties.com. Most people will not remember your name, but if they are looking for a property on the lake, they will probably remember your website. Alternatively, if they enter these terms into a search engine, they will probably find you quite easily. Also, be sure to reference your website URL on all your traditional marketing. This drives more traffic to your site. Your business cards, brochures, newspaper ads, postcards, mailers, etc. should all have your web branding and website address.

If you service different niches, create different URLs for each niche. This allows you to direct web visitors to specific areas based upon their interests. For example, if one of your niches is representing first time buyers, you could use AustinFirstTimeHomeBuyers.com or AustinBuyers.com. Remember, people are poor at remembering names and much more likely to find you if you reference your location, a term that references real estate, and a specific niche you service.

Capture Your Neighborhood

To capture more neighborhood business, set up a neighborhood website. Prospects are more likely to buy from someone with whom they share similarities. When people meet strangers, one of the first methods they use to build connection is to determine where the other person lives. When both parties live in the same neighborhood, an instantaneous bond often forms. To capitalize on this, create a neighborhood website for the community where you live.

Neighborhood websites create an on-line community where neighbors can exchange information and post upcoming events such as birthdays or block parties, etc. These websites also contain neighborhood-specific content, including school data, recreational activities, Chamber of Commerce information, local weather, etc. The agent markets their services by hosting the site. Given today's hectic pace, many people find it easier to connect electronically than in person. Neighbors can share pictures, announce upcoming neighborhood events, share recipes, as well as other important data. Most neighborhood website providers monitor content so nothing inappropriate appears on-line.

To implement this strategy, determine if this service is available in your area. If so, begin your campaign using traditional postcard techniques or letters inviting neighbors to preview the site. The site displays your picture and contact information so visitors know who is sponsoring the service. If you are doing telephone or face-to-face prospecting, invite the people you talk with to visit the site and check out the resources. While they are at your neighborhood site, you can ask them to answer the question of the month. For example, ask them to share their favorite gardening tips, recipes, ideas for holiday decorations, etc. You could also host a neighbor appreciation event where everyone brings a favorite dish for a potluck luncheon. The same approach would also work with people who attend your place of worship, as well as members of your alumni association or other types of clubs.

No matter what strategy you use, your goal is to have people connect with each other as well as with you as their agent. Remember, most people do business with the first agent who contacts them. Hosting a neighborhood website keeps your name top of mind as both a neighbor and as the neighborhood real estate professional.

Capture the Property Address

An excellent strategy few agents employ is setting up a separate website using the property address as the URL. For example, if you are listing 123 Main Street in Smithville, you can obtain 123MainStreetSmithville.com. This makes it easy for potential buyers to remember where to see the property on the web. Even better, when the new buyers want to list, if you own the URL, the buyers will have an additional motivation to use you as their listing agent.

Reports from the Field
This Is SO Far above the Others, We're Using You!
Jerry Rossi, RossiSpeaks.com
Raleigh, North Carolina

Most agents post listings on their own website, on their company's website, and on Realtor.com. Over the last several years, third level domain websites have become quite popular. For example, if I take a listing at 123 Main Street, I would create a third level domain website for the seller's listing. The URL (web address) for the site would be 123MainStreet-RossiRealty.com.

A company called AgencyLogic.com has created the next generation of websites using this concept. This tool allows you to create a website for each of your listings using the property address as the URL. For example, the property at 123 Main Street would be listed as www.123MainStreetRaleighNC.com. The website takes only a few minutes to prepare. All you need to do is choose the template you want, type a brief property description, and upload some digital photos of the property.

Prior to going on the listing presentation, I also like to prepare a sign rider that has the property URL on it. Instead of using a brochure box, the sign rider refers buyers to the website at www.123MainStreetRaleighNC.com. I obtain a blank sign rider and work with a software program from MyCustomSigns.com to print the address for the sign using my own computer.

On a recent listing appointment, the sellers were ready to list with another agent. Using the AgencyLogic.com software, it took only a few minutes to create a website that was the focal point of the listing presentation. The live, on-line demonstration of the seller's website during the listing presentation included digital pictures of the property, information about local schools, a map to the property, a mortgage calculator, a property brochure, and a floor plan.

All that was required to make the website go "live" was a push of the button. The sellers' response was:

This is so far above the others, we're using you!

They cancelled the other appointments they had and listed the property at a full commission.

After the property closes, we give the website as a gift to the new homeowner. This allows the buyers to show their friends and family their new home. They can upload additional pictures of the property, their children, or of anything else. The domain expires after six months and the homeowner bears the cost from that time forward. The beauty of this is that the buyers often like this gift so much that they will list with us when they are ready to sell. In addition to increasing both listings and referrals, each site links back to my site. This drives more traffic to our websites and improves our search engine ranking as well!

Immediacy: The Most Important
Weapon in Your Arsenal

No matter what type of web strategy you elect, web visitors want the information NOW. The following statistics from Real Estate Connect (July 2004) outline what web visitors expect:

1. Twenty-five percent expect instantaneous response.
2. Fifty percent expect follow-up in two hours.
3. One hundred percent expect follow-up within one business day.

If you do not respond rapidly, the visitor will be gone. In terms of your competitors, however, if you respond quickly to e-mail and web inquiries, you have a high probability of winning the client's business. Remember, 73 percent of all sellers do business with the first agent with whom they speak. In terms of responding quickly, our industry's performance in this area is poor.

1. Fifty-eight percent do not respond at all.
2. Of the agents who do respond, 70 percent take at least two days to respond.

If you are unable to respond quickly, hire an assistant to handle the initial contact for you. Alternatively, instruct your web visitors to call your 800 Call Capture system to reach you immediately. Remember, if you're the first agent to speak to the lead, you have a very high probability they will do business with you.

Chapter 9 Supporting Scripts

Marketing on the web will be critical to real estate success now and in the future. Realtor.com has been tracking what properties are most attractive to web visitors. Their data show that most visitors skip over listings with only one picture and concentrate on properties that have multiple pictures and/or a virtual tour. Posting at least ten digital pictures and a virtual tour on numerous websites is an excellent way to develop business from the web. Remember, there are at least six places you can post your listings to the web. These include Realtor.com, your company's national website, your personal website, your office website, a neighborhood website, plus a website with the property address as the URL. This strategy maximizes the seller's web exposure. Quick response time for both e-mail and Call Capture inquiries means buyers learn about the property when they are most interested—at the time they make their inquiry. The scripts below will help you articulate this for the seller during your listing consultation.

Script #1: Plenty of pictures

An excellent way to make your property stand out on the web is with a virtual tour plus at least ten digital pictures. Research from Realtor.com, the most visited real estate website, shows that visitors skip over properties with only one picture. In contrast, properties with a virtual tour plus multiple photos receive the most attention. Is having a virtual tour plus multiple photos of your property on the web a service you want?

Script #2: Maximum exposure

In order to obtain the highest price possible for your property, having maximum exposure on the web is important. If you decide to list with me, your property will appear with at least ten digital photos and a virtual tour on six different websites. The six websites are Realtor.com, my company's national website, my office's local website, my personal website, and a neighborhood website that I host. In addition, I will set up a separate website with your property address as the URL or web address. Is having your property listed on six different websites a service you want?

(You can alter the script above to reflect the services you provide and insert your own URLs in the scripts below.)

Script #3: Neighborhood website

Did you know that many properties sell because a neighbor in the area knows someone who would like to live here? To capitalize on this fact, I host a neighborhood website where I will post your property for sale. Have you had a chance to visit My NeighborhoodWebsite.com?

Wait for their response. Then continue:

Would you be interested in seeing how your property will appear on the site?

If "Yes," demonstrate how their home would look.
If "No," continue by asking,

Is having your property posted on my neighborhood website a service you want?

Script #4: Your home website

I have prepared a separate website that uses your property address as the website address. Would you like a demonstration of what your property's website would be like should you list with me?

Wait for their response. If "Yes," demonstrate the site.

The beauty of this website is that buyers can see your property 24 hours a day, seven days a week without ever having to disturb you. Better yet, all I have to do is press a button to activate your website right now and we'll start marketing your property on the web immediately. Is marketing your property using the street address a service you want?

Each of the strategies above can help you overcome the discount objection. If you use Script #4, the sellers are often so excited about having a unique website that they will list on the spot.

Chapter 9 Action Plan

According to an article in *Inman News* on January 20, 2005, "Three quarters of consumers now start the home search process online, while only about 11 percent of advertising dollars are currently spent on the Web." According to the 2004 NAR Profile of Home Buyers and Sellers, 74 percent of all buyers used the Internet in their search while only 53 percent used the newspaper. If you are relying on the newspaper exclusively, you are missing the opportunities available from advertising on the Internet.

Whether you a beginner or a sophisticated web marketer, the action steps below can help you generate more leads from your website. As in previous chapters, place a plus (**+**) next to each item you plan to implement in your business. Prioritize the items and remember to avoid trying to make too many changes at once. Start with what is easiest for you to implement. Again, small changes over time yield huge results. See Appendix A for additional web marketing resources.

Action Steps

____ 1. I will change my website from being agent-centric to being client-centric.

____ 2. In order to determine if my website is easy to navigate, I will watch a friend or relative who is not computer savvy view my website. If this person has difficulty, I will change my website to make it easier to navigate.

____ 3. I will allow web visitors to opt in to the services I provide through my site rather than forcing them to register against their will.

____ 4. I will set up my website so it accesses the MLS through IDX (Internet Data Exchange) or VOW (Virtual Office Website).

____ 5. I will create a call to action that motivates my web visitors to provide their personal contact information. The call to action could be a complimentary CMA by telephone, free newsletter, free on-line class, or other service.

____ 6. I will create a new web address that is easy to remember and references function rather than my name.

____ 7. I will respond to all web inquiries on the same day they are received or hire someone to do this for me.

____ 8. I will place my 800 Call Capture number on my website.

____ 9. I will host a neighborhood website.

____10. I will create a separate website with the property address as the URL for each of my listings.

To convert more leads from your websites, you must have web traffic. One of the best ways to drive traffic to your website is using the search engines.

Chapter 10
Winning the Web Campaign:
Rev Up Your Search Engines

Know thy enemy and know thy self
and you will win a hundred battles.
—Sun Tzu Wu

What I do now and what I will add to my business:

Put a checkmark (√) next to what you do now. Leave the remaining items blank. Review the action steps at the end of the chapter to determine the strategies you will implement in your business.

_____ 1. My website is optimized for search engine placement.

_____ 2. My website has a site map.

_____ 3. I have asked other businesses to link to my website.

_____ 4. I participate in a pay-per-click program.

_____ 5. The company I work for has a first place ranking on at least two major search engines (Yahoo, Google, or MSN).

_____ 6. I use Alexa rankings as part of my listing consultation.

Putting Your Website to Work

Once you have a killer website that motivates web visitors to contact you, you must also address web marketing and search engine placement. The most effective way to meet this challenge is to hire a search engine specialist to handle this on your behalf. Your job is to be in front of buyers and sellers—not spending time trying to figure out how to increase your web placement. To drive more traffic to your personal website, you will need to address a variety of issues.

1. *Key word phrases and metatags*

   The best website providers optimize your website by packing it with key word phrases and metatags. "Key word phrases" describe what your site provides to your web visitors. For example, if your niche is selling probate properties in Austin, Texas, you could brand your site as austinprobatesellers.com. Key word phrases would include, "Austin," "Texas," "real estate," "probate," "probate sellers," "probate listings," "probate buyers," etc. Your web designer will also incorporate these key phrases as "metatags" in the code the search engine reads. Metatags are visible to the search engines, but are not visible to your web visitors.

2. *Site map*

   Site maps also enhance search engine placement and may appear at the bottom of your home page. In other cases, the site map is elsewhere but easily accessible to the search engines such as Yahoo and Google. Search engines "spider" the web by searching the Internet for phrases that closely match the requested search. The search engine ranks the results based upon how closely the website matches the search. Spidering search engines target site maps, read them, and then match their searches based upon what is on the map.

3. *Link popularity*

   A different strategy is link popularity. This refers to how many other sites link back to your site. A great way to increase your link popularity is to ask other businesses or agents who are not geographical competitors to link to your site in exchange for you linking to their site. Link popularity also helps you achieve higher placement.

Gobble Up the Competition with Google

Search engine placement (i.e., where your website ranks in comparison to other websites) is best left to experts unless you enjoy spending long hours trying to determine mathematical formulas for web placement.

Understanding the basics of how search engine placement works, however, can give you a huge competitive advantage.

Website rankings are constantly in flux, often changing each time you do a search. Your ranking is contingent upon traffic, pay-per-clicks, as well as whatever algorithm (formula) the search engine companies are using to provide ranking.

Google currently is the most widely used search engine for real estate searches. Google not only provides data for their own searches, they also offer this service for a number of other Internet providers, such as AOL. In fact, unless you are searching MSN or Yahoo, Google probably is the source feeding the search engine you are using.

The Google Dance

Obtaining great search engine placement is akin to predicting the future with a crystal ball. The search engine companies do not publicize how they establish their rankings. Complicating matters, they constantly change their criteria so even the full time professionals are usually guessing. Web professionals who spend their days trying to decipher how Google ranks sites have termed this the "Google Dance."

Location, Location, Location

If you are going to compete effectively against discounters by using the web, location is everything. In this case, location means placement on the first page of the search. An important step in revving up your engines is to determine your company's ranking on the major search engines. If you have a personal website, where does it rank? To determine your website rankings, follow the steps below.

Begin by opening the search engine you want to use. Once the search window comes up, type in the name of your city (or local marketplace) as well as the words "real estate" or "homes." For example, if you live in Portland, Oregon, you would type in "Portland Oregon real estate" or "Portland Oregon homes." Be sure to use the quotation marks since this tells the search engine you want that specific phrase.

Once your search comes up, you will notice several different types of information on the page. On some pages, you will see two or three sponsored links at the top of the page. These advertisers are usually large institutions that pay sizeable fees for top placement. HomeGain,

Service Magic, and Lending Tree are often in these spots since they buy millions of dollars of web advertising annually.

Directly below the space for the top two or three sponsored results, you will see the balance of the pay-per-click results. These advertisements have priority over people who do not pay for web placement. Pay-per-click works much like an auction. The more you bid per click, the better your placement. Advertisers normally set a monthly budget. When advertisers reach their budgeted figure, the search engine drops them until they either replenish their account or until the following month. As a result, search engine rankings constantly change.

Beneath the pay-per-click advertisers, the search engines then rank the websites best matching your search based upon its formula for determining which websites best match your search request.

As you look at the results of your search, also note the advertisements in the margin. This area is a combination of pay-per-click and traditional print advertising. Unlike the search areas, this area posts short ads much like the classified ads in a newspaper. The cost for the ad is based upon how many visitors click through to your website.

Positioning Yourself for Victory

If you are affiliated with a major local or national brand, does your company's website appear on the first page of the major search engines? If so, does your site rank higher than your competitors' sites? If your company does not appear on the first page, the next question is which of your competitors are listed? If your site or your company's site comes up ahead of the competition, you can incorporate this competitive advantage into your listing consultation. If not, your lack of web placement puts you at a serious competitive disadvantage.

The More You Spend, the Better Your Position

In most cases, the easiest way to show up on the front page of the major search engines is through their paid advertising programs. As an agent, you have two options. The first option is to create a classified ad much like a newspaper ad. Most search engines ads cannot exceed three lines and approximately 100 characters. Before writing your ad, look at the other ads, especially those in major metropolitan areas. This will give you some ideas about the type of ad you can place. Also, remember to make your ad about the consumer as well as identifying the geographical region and niche you service.

You can also purchase key words or key phrases. As with the ads, when someone types in a key word or phrase, the search engine provides rankings based upon who paid the most for placement. The only time advertisers are charged is when someone clicks through to their website. All search engines list paid ads first and then list the remaining sites based upon the formula the company uses for web placement. Google, MSN, Yahoo, Overture, and Looksmart, plus numerous other companies, offer pay-per-click services. The popularity of the key word phrases determines the pricing. The more popular the phrase, the higher the bidding will be. Check with your search engine specialist to learn how to achieve the best Google and Overture placement.

A key point to remember is that there are approximately 25 to 30 positions available on the first page of most searches. Web visitors rarely scroll past the second page of any search. What this means is that competition for these spots will continue to increase and as a result, will become more expensive. If you can obtain top positioning, do so. If it is out of your price range, consider designing several websites that are specific to a neighborhood, subdivision, or market niche such as golf course properties or teachers.

Caveat #1:
There is no point in doing a pay-per-click program unless your website motivates your web visitors to contact you. If your website does not provide an incentive for web visitors to contact you or if you do not respond rapidly to web leads, you are wasting your money.

Caveat #2:
Be wary of companies that offer you top placement on the major search engines. There are approximately 10 to 15 spots based upon the search criteria and another 7 to 10 spots for advertisers. If you are in a large metropolitan area, it will be difficult to obtain top placement without spending exorbitant amounts of money. A better alternative is to use specific subdivisions or names of condominium complexes when creating your key words, metatags, and pay-per-click search words.

Search engines charge a fixed fee each time someone clicks through to your website. The larger the market is, the more expensive the ad will be. Before submitting an ad, most search engines allow you to determine both cost and approximate search placement. Once again, hiring an experienced search engine specialist is the most effective way to meet this challenge.

The strategies for achieving great placement change constantly since the major search engines are always altering how they rank sites. Again, an experienced search engine specialist can target your market so you generate the most leads from your advertising.

If You Can't Beat 'Em, Join 'Em

If you are with a small company or if your company has poor web placement, there is another option you may want to consider. Specifically, go to Google, MSN, and Yahoo and type in the name of the geographical area where you sell real estate. For example, to search for information on Austin real estate, you would type any of the following phrases: "Austin real estate," "Austin homes," "Austin properties," "Austin Texas real estate," etc.

Next, see which companies come up at the top of the first page of your search. If one of the lead generation companies such as HomeGain or Service Magic comes up, consider becoming a member, especially if your company fails to make the first page of the search. Most lead generation companies charge a flat fee per lead or for membership. The leads are predominantly buyers unless you are paying a flat rate for seller leads. Even if you are a listing agent, however, being a member may allow you to be the first agent to reach the perfect buyer for your listing.

A key point to remember is 73 percent of sellers who close transactions do so with the first agent they contact. Belonging to a lead generation company increases the probability you will be that first contact. In terms of which lead generation companies to join, at the time this book went to press, HomeGain had more web traffic than any other real estate company website with the exception of Realtor.com.

The next strategy works well if you belong to a major national firm or are with a large, local independent. It does not work well if your company has a mediocre website or very little web traffic.

Meet Alexa: A Not-So-Secret Secret Weapon

Sellers want maximum exposure on the web. To compare your company's web traffic with that of your competitors, visit www.Alexa.com. Alexa tells you where your company's website (or your personal website) ranks against the over 4,000,000 websites they track. If you are in the top 100,000, you are doing well since this places you in the top 2.5 percent of the sites they track. Billions of other sites do not even make the Alexa ranking system. Alexa allows you to see if your traffic is increasing or decreasing. It also shows how many unique visitors you have per million hits (reach) as well as how long Alexa users spend on your website (page views).

To utilize this secret weapon, visit www.Alexa.com and type in your company's website address (URL). Alexa will generate a traffic ranking for your company's site. (You can use this tool for your personal website as well.) Next, click on "traffic details." This will take you to the site's latest web rankings. In terms of what the ranking means, the lower your number, the higher your web traffic. For example, Yahoo is one, MSN is two, Google is four, the Weather Channel is usually in the mid 200s, and Realtor.com usually is about 300. The major real estate brands range from 4,000 to 20,000. If you are ranked in the top 100,000 sites, Alexa will generate a chart like the one in Table 2.

Table 2

Coldwell Banker

coldwellbanker.com

Commercial and residential brokerage with franchises throughout the US, Canada, and Europe; includes searchable database of listings, mortgage options, details on services, and a directory of local offices.

Traffic Rank for coldwellbanker.com: 5,442

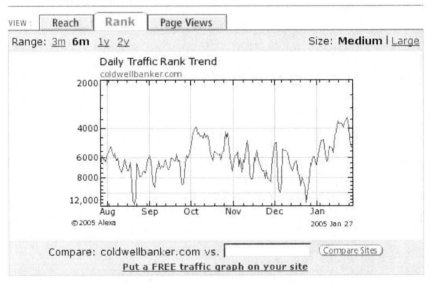

Table 3

To determine how your company's site compares to the competition, type your competitor's web address in the box where it says, "Compare sites." This resulting graphic below shows how your company's ranking and web traffic compares against competitors who also appear in the top 100,000.

(Please note CB is the top line and RE/MAX is the bottom line.)

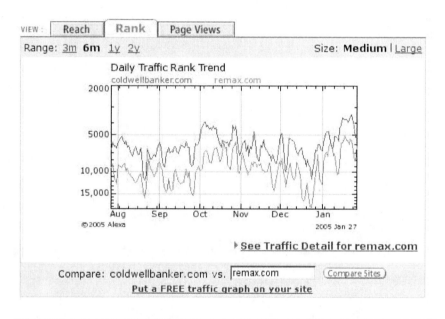

Table 4

You can also use the Alexa traffic rankings to compare how many web visitors your site reaches per million Alexa website hits.

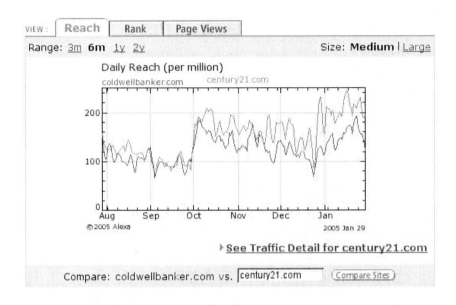

The great thing about this tool is that Alexa is an objective source that illustrates how your site and your competitor's site compare in terms of the number of visitors and page views. At the time we went to press, the only two discounters in the top 50,000 were Help-U-Sell and Foxtons. In contrast, most discounters rank between 1 million and 4 million. What this means is these websites have very little traffic. Remember, your goal is to help the seller achieve the highest possible price for their property in the shortest possible time. To do this, the seller must have maximum exposure on the web. When a competitor's website has poor ranking, the seller is NOT receiving maximum exposure to the marketplace. This translates into a lower purchase price.

I Used to Work for an On-line Discounter
Adrian Willanger, Windermere Real Estate Lake Forest Park
Seattle, Washington

I used to work for an on-line discounter. It was a tremendous experience. I received an amazing education about how to market on the web. At the time, the company had the best technology in the industry. Due to their superior technology, they believed that people would flock to their way of doing business. Their commission structure was 3 percent to the buyer's agent and 1.5 percent to the listing agent. Their model had two primary challenges. First, they focused on the technology rather than on real estate. Second, they ignored the fact the real estate is a people business. As a result, they went bankrupt.

The most important lesson I learned from the on-line discount company was the importance of marketing to specific market niches. The web has become so compartmentalized, you must specialize in order to succeed. I have four different websites that target four very different markets. My websites include: WhatsItWorth.biz; SeattleHomestyle.com; LuxuryHomesInSeattle.com; and IdahoHomestyle.com. I use E-Agent.biz to generate leads.

When I do a listing presentation, I give sellers a list of the services I provide. This includes a strong e-mail marketing program, web-marketing program, and traditional marketing program. Moreover, I emphasize that I take hundreds of clock hours of training each year to be a good practitioner. Sellers clearly get more by listing with me. I'm in a position to earn good fees because of the broad range of services I provide.

Do people ask me to discount? The answer is almost never. When they do, I firmly tell them "No." If they persist, I give them an even stronger "NO!" If they really want an agent who will discount their fee, I'm not attached. I thank them for their time and I leave. In most cases, when I stand up to walk away, the sellers normally say, "We had to try."

Sometimes a seller will ask me to reduce my fee when we sell their home quickly. My response is, "The reason you sold your home fast is I'm the best. The hardest part is closing the transaction. Because so many sales do not close, you definitely want me on your side."

Sellers work with me because they get more than they would with a discount broker. Because of this, I haven't discounted a commission for years.

Chapter 10 Supporting Scripts

Many people still are not web savvy. For them, a discussion of web marketing should be short and simple. In contrast, your web savvy sellers will expect you to have a sophisticated discussion about how you will market on the web. The scripts below will help you work effectively with both groups. Select the scripts you will use based upon your style of doing business and how closely the script fits your clients' level of sophistication. Trying to explain too much to sellers who may not be that sophisticated can confuse them.

Script #1: Clients are not web savvy and your company has high web placement.

To reach as many buyers as possible ,one of the most important places to market is on the Internet. As you can see from this Alexa.com chart, ABC Realty does more business on the Internet than our competitors do. Better exposure on the web translates into more money for you. Is having maximum exposure for your property on the Internet a service you want?

Regardless of how they answer, move on to the next part of your consultation. Sellers who are not familiar with the web generally respond better to traditional advertising campaigns. Adjust your consultation accordingly.

Script #2: Clients are web savvy and your company has high web placement

Having a strong presence on the Internet is critical to helping you achieve the highest price possible for your property. As you can see from these three searches on Google, MSN, and Yahoo, our company comes up at the top of each search.

Give copies to the sellers. Continue the conversation by saying:

Is being listed with the company that ranks highly on the search engines a service you want?

Script #3: Pay-per-click program

To make sure your property has maximum exposure on the web, I use a pay-per-click program to advertise on Google, MSN, and Yahoo. This increases the probability that web visitors will see your property.

Depending upon your placement, give a copy of your searches to the sellers. Continue the conversation by saying:

Is being listed with an agent who has a strong web advertising program a service you want?

Script #4: Agent belongs to lead generation company* and company has high web ranking on Alexa.com

*Note: Substitute the name of any lead generation companies to which you belong.

Having a strong presence on the web is critical to helping you achieve the highest price possible for your property. As you can see from these web traffic comparison charts from Alexa.com, our company generates more web leads than our competitors generate.

Hand out the traffic comparison charts from Alexa.com.

In addition, I also belong to a lead generation company called HomeGain. As you can see from the Alexa traffic analysis, HomeGain generates more web visitors than any real estate company in our area. This means that if you list with me, your property will have maximum exposure to buyer leads for this area. Is having maximum exposure to buyer leads a service you want?

Script #5: Company and agent have low web rankings; agent belongs to lead generation company

Having a strong presence on the web is critical to helping you achieve the highest price possible for your property. I belong to a lead generation company called HomeGain that generates more web leads than any major real estate company.

Hand out the traffic comparison charts from Alexa.com.

This means that if you list with me, your property will have maximum exposure to buyer leads for this area. Is having maximum exposure to buyer leads a service you want?

Chapter 10 Action Plan

Have you started using the web to build your business? If not, the transition is not as difficult as you may think. It's true that web optimization, search engine placement, and pay-per-clicks can be daunting. The secret to implementing a strong web marketing campaign is to take it a step at a time. If your present company has strong search engine placement, you already have a strong competitive advantage you can use during your listing consultation. If not, you can join a lead generation company like HomeGain that has first page web placement in a multitude of markets nationwide.

You can improve your personal search engine placement by using the strategies below. Keep in mind that your website is there to support the other advertising you do. It is not a substitute for signs, print advertising, or door knocking. It is simply a way of reaching more people across a wider geographical area.

You will find additional resources in Appendix A. Place a plus (+) next to each item you plan to implement in your business. Rewrite any action steps that need alteration. Remember, take one step at a time. Do what is easiest first and then add items when you can. If you make only one change each month from the list below, you will complete all eight action steps in a little over six months.

Action Steps

_____ 1. I will speak to my website designer to determine how to optimize my website for search engine placement.

_____ 2. I will check with my web designer to determine whether there is a site map on my website. If not, I will ask the web designer to add a site map within the next two weeks.

_____ 3. As part of my lead generation program, I will ask other businesses to exchange links with me.

_____ 4. When I meet agents outside my immediate service area, I will ask them to exchange links with me.

_____ 5. I will hire a search engine specialist to implement a pay-per-click program for my business.

_____ 6. If my company ranks well on the major search engines, I will show sellers how this helps them obtain the highest possible price for their property.

_____ 7. I will join a lead generation company so I can show sellers how I generate buyer leads from the web.

_____ 8. I will use Alexa rankings as a regular part of my listing consultation.

The Internet has made it possible for agents to serve clients from all over the world. To WOW your sellers on your next listing consultation, show them how you market their property globally, not just locally.

Chapter 11
Winning the Web Campaign: Ditch Discounters with a Global Marketing Plan

*As consumers we get more demanding all the time.
We want better quality. We want it faster. And cheaper.
Plus, we want more choices. Whoever comes along
that can satisfy all these "wants" gets our business.*
                                    —Price Pritchett

What I do now and what I will add to my business:

Put a checkmark (√) next to what you do now. Leave the remaining items blank. Review the action steps at the end of the chapter to determine the strategies you will implement in your business.

_____ 1. I work for a company with a national relocation service.

_____ 2. I work for a company with an international relocation service.

_____ 3. I am fluent in at least one other language besides English.

_____ 4. One of my niches is marketing to people who are fluent in a language other than English.

_____ 5. In my service area, the MLS I belong to is available in other languages in addition to English.

Create an International Marketing Strategy

To increase the probability of winning the discount war, you must have a strategy that extends not only locally and nationally, but internationally as well. With the exception of Help-U-Sell, Assist2Sell, and some For-Sale-by-Owner sites, most discounters are local. Chapter 9 discussed strategies for driving business to your website. A global marketing plan allows you to reach a much broader audience. If you want to ditch discounters, using international web marketing strategies is an excellent way to do it.

National and International Trumps Local When It Comes to Relocation

Most communities have a steady stream of relocation sellers and buyers. If you are with a major national firm, you already have three important advantages when it comes to reaching relocation or other out of area buyers:

Advantage #1:

Relocation buyers generally begin their web searches with companies they know. While a large independent may dominate the local market, someone moving from out of area will check the websites of nationally recognized firms. This is especially true when one of the firms is the dominant player in their local market. Thus, having your listings posted to a national real estate website increases the probability that national and international relocation buyers will see your listings first.

Advantage #2:

Large national companies also command a bigger piece of the relocation pie. Because they have offices in most cities, companies whose employees are relocating are more likely to select a major brand to assist with their relocation needs. The major brands have full-blown relocation departments devoted exclusively to handling relocation clientele. These companies are accustomed to dealing with specific relocation issues and hence provide the relocation client a higher level of service. Most relocation companies also prefer working with national firms for the same reasons.

Advantage #3

Most major national firms also have an international presence. This translates into increased international traffic since buyers already know these companies. Companies that have both a national and international presence create a better relocation experience by providing expert assistance both inside and outside the country. This makes coping with international relocation challenges more manageable. In contrast, a seller who lists with a local discounter will generally have little, if any, exposure to this lucrative market. Regardless of whether or not you work for a major company, you can capture international leads in a wide variety of ways.

Most Agents Look at Us
Like We're a Lab Experiment

Don Schoeller, Owner OrlandoRelocation.com
Orlando, Florida

Our niche is marketing exclusively to relocation buyers for Orlando. We do not overall take listings. Since we have people relocating here from all over the world, our brokerage is international. My team and I were among the very first agents in Florida to begin marketing on the web. Over the last year, we generated over 3,000 leads. I have three buyers' agents and refer a substantial amount of business as well.

Orlando was once primarily a vacation destination. Today, it's one of the strongest technology centers in the country. It is also one of the hottest real estate markets in the country, attracting huge numbers of high-tech professionals. These high-tech up-scale buyers expect their agent to be technologically sophisticated.

Most clients do a substantial percentage of their shopping prior to the time they arrive in Orlando. This region of Florida used to be quite inexpensive. People are surprised to find this is no longer the case. The advantage of using the web is that it eliminates sticker shock before buyers arrive. It also allows buyers who cannot afford the prices to withdraw gracefully. Because buyers do most of their homework on the web, it usually takes only one day to find them a home.

There's a nuclear war going on out there for listings. The competition is brutal. In contrast, our Internet leads all say the same thing: "You're the only agent who contacted us or showed a serious interest in providing the level of service we required." The e-mail leads keep flowing in and so do the closings. While other agents struggle with discounting, most sellers happily pay three percent to an agent with a qualified buyer. Discounting is not a major issue for our business model yet. What's ironic is how agents react to what we do. When I describe our business model, most agents look at us like we're a lab experiment.

Before we agree to work with an Internet buyer, we determine whether they meet our standards. If not, we refer them to another agent. Our standards include being pre-qualified. This means I must speak directly to their lender or receive a mortgage intent letter to verify there is nothing in the file that would prevent them from obtaining a loan. We also don't work with buyers who must sell their existing property prior to purchasing. If they do not bring their checkbook ready to purchase, we don't have time to work with them. Our retention ratio is extremely high and we close virtually everything we put a contract on. Also our average ticket sale price is more than twice the median average price in our market.

This new breed of Internet Empowered Consumer is demanding and we must embrace change whether we like it or not. To stay on top, we constantly research how the relocation buyer is searching the web. Wherever the buyers are, that's where we must be.

Plan Today to Win Tomorrow

Experts predict that by 2010, over 65 percent of first-time buyers will be immigrants or minorities. This means a majority of our future clients may not speak English as their first language. For example, in the Los Angeles Unified School District students speak more than 60 different languages. Furthermore, over 60 percent of the students are Hispanic. With this tremendous increase in diversity, how can you effectively market to global buyers and sellers in a way that differentiates you from the competition? When you wage war internationally rather than just locally, you effectively eliminate discounters since most have no presence in this rapidly growing market segment.

Global Website Strategy

Most immigrants and foreign consumers appreciate an agent who genuinely cares about their needs. Even better, global clients tend to refer other global clients. To market effectively in a global environment, follow the guidelines below.

1. As mentioned in Chapter 9, a killer website engages the visitor with a series of offers, reports, and other useful information. To capture a share of the global market, you must become fluent in another language or partner with someone who is fluent. The next step is to translate your key web pages into the other language. Be sure to have the translation carefully proofed by a native speaker. At the top of your English web page, add a line that says, "I speak your language" and reference the links to the translated pages.

2. Most global buyers are accustomed to paying all cash for a property or at least making a substantial down payment. Mortgage practices vary dramatically across the world. You can capture global visitors by translating mortgage information and requirements for qualification, including qualifications for people who may not be United States residents. For foreign sellers, be sure to check the state and federal FIRPTA (Foreign Investment in Real Estate Property Tax Act) requirements.

3. If possible, translate Chamber of Commerce information on schools, proximity to transportation, employment opportunities, recreation, etc. Whatever you have translated into other languages will assist you in building an international, multi-lingual clientele.

4. Whether you are dealing with a relocation buyer from 50 miles away or 5,000 miles away, it is critical to explain how transactions are negotiated and closed in your area. North America is a hodgepodge of different closing practices that include escrow, attorneys, and title companies. Buyers need to know what to expect. Many foreign buyers take title using their company's name, especially if their company does business in the U.S. If this is the case, consult an attorney or title company expert about what your region requires.

5. Realtor.com reports the number one priority for their web visitors is having as many pictures as possible. Since out of area buyers rely on virtual tours to identify what they want to see, provide as many photos as possible, especially for your own listings.

6. Know what your global buyers want. For example, many Asian buyers will not purchase a house with a "4" in the address. (Four sounds like the word for death.) Eights are lucky. Better yet, work with a Feng Shui expert to make the house appealing to Asian buyers.

Global MLS Strategy

Even if you do not speak a foreign language, another terrific alternative for attracting global buyers is www.Immobel.com. Immobel.com provides complete translations of MLS databases into the viewers' choice of 12 languages. This service is available to both Realtor® Associations and to individual agents in certain areas. For those agents whose MLS provides this service (this includes Florida, large parts of Texas, North Carolina, Southern California, Las Vegas, Chicago, New Orleans, as well as a number of other cities), all agents have to do is ask their MLS to turn on the service and give them the link. If the MLS does not provide the service, the individual agent still may be able to use Immobel's technology.

To see how this looks on the main MLS website in English and then view what a visitor who speaks Spanish would see, visit www.Immobel.com and scroll through the various pages in the navigation bar.

Immobel.com allows agents to link this data to their personal websites. This allows visitors to view local MLS information in their native language. Properties may be listed in languages other than English as well. Visitors can view Paris properties in English, Florida properties in Spanish, San Francisco properties in Chinese, and so on around the world. In addition, this powerful tool also allows you to preview properties in Europe and Australia.

The ability to provide global buyers and sellers with information in their native language can be a tremendous marketing tool. As the demographics of your customer base change, adjusting how you market your services to people who do not speak English will give you a huge advantage over competitors whose only strategy is to reduce the commission.

Chapter 11 Supporting Scripts

Marketing nationally and internationally on the web ensures the largest pool of potential buyers will view the seller's property. Having the MLS information available in 12 different languages allows broader exposure to buyers locally, nationally, and internationally. The scripts below articulate how to incorporate a global marketing strategy into your listing consultation.

Script #1: National or international relocation
Due to the international nature of the Internet, we are experiencing an increase of both national and international buyers. My company offers relocation services to buyers both inside and outside the United States. Because of these services, more buyers will visit our company website and use our company to relocate. The more exposure your listing has, the higher the price. Is having access to national and international buyers a service you want?

Script #2: Marketing to buyers who do not speak English*
*If you speak a language other than Spanish or if another language is spoken by a large number of people in your market area, adapt this script accordingly.

Many buyers in our marketplace speak languages other than English. To reach this growing segment of the market, I provide my services in Spanish. Would you like to see the Spanish version of my website?

Wait for their response. If "Yes," demonstrate your website. If "No," continue the conversation by asking,

Is reaching as many buyers as possible a service you want?

Script #3: Multiple Listing Service available in twelve languages
When buyers visit a real estate website, the link they click on the most often is the link to the Multiple Listing Service. I subscribe to a special service that translates our Multiple Listing Service into 12 different languages. This means visitors to my website can view your listing in 12 different languages. Is having your property description available in multiple languages a service you want?

Chapter 11 Action Plan

If you work for one of the major real estate companies or have an affiliation with a large relocation company, you may already have a global marketing plan. If you haven't done so already, investigate your company's relocation department and determine whether they provide national or international services. The next step is to incorporate this into your listing consultation as one of the key points of differentiation.

Even if your company lacks a relocation department, you can still market globally by using the technology tools from this chapter. Having the MLS available in a number of languages will be a major point of differentiation that is extremely attractive to a wide array of sellers and buyers. This is especially true for the estates market where your high probability buyers may be from outside the country.

If you are not fluent in at least two languages, consider purchasing a language program on audio CD that you can listen to in your car. This is one of the easiest ways to learn a new language. It also has the extra benefit of taking your mind off the traffic.

Remember to place a plus (**+**) next to each item you plan to implement in your business and place them in priority order. Leave the other items blank. Rewrite any action steps that need alteration. See Appendix A for Resources you can use.

Action Steps

____ 1. In future listing consultations, I will discuss how my company's national relocation service assists sellers in obtaining the highest possible price for their property.

____ 2. If my company provides international relocation, I will show sellers how national and international relocation attracts more buyers.

____ 3. I will listen to audio CDs or take classes to become fluent in another language.

____ 4. I will create a niche by marketing my services to people who are fluent in languages other than English.

___ 5. I will set up at least one page on my website in another language.

___ 6. I will investigate whether my MLS has the ability to post MLS information in other languages. If so, I will make this service available on my website.

___ 7. If my MLS is not available in other languages, I will individually subscribe to the service to make it available on my website.

Whether it's from traditional or web marketing, the service you provide to potential sellers will determine whether they will list with you. An excellent way to win the seller is by helping them stage their home.

Chapter 12
Winning the Customer Service Campaign: Setting the Stage for Victory

A gem cannot be polished without friction,
nor a person perfected without trials.
—Confucius

What I do now and what I will add to my business:
Put a checkmark (√) next to what you do now. Leave the remaining items blank. Review the action steps at the end of the chapter to determine the strategies you will implement in your business.

___ 1. I provide sellers with a list of suggestions to help them make their property more attractive to buyers.

___ 2. I personally assist sellers in staging their property and offer this service during my listing consultation.

___ 3. I work with a professional decorator who assists sellers in presenting their properties to best advantage.

___ 4. I provide sellers with a list of Feng Shui tips to help them sell their home more quickly.

___ 5. I refer sellers to a Feng Shui specialist to assist them in staging their homes for a quick sale.

"All the World's a Stage"

Shakespeare's famous quote, "All the world's a stage…" is certainly apropos in the real estate business. Homes presented to their best advantage bring maximum purchase prices. Staging involves making the house look as good as possible, often with minimal cost. It is also an excellent strategy to differentiate your services from those of your competitors. Staging takes place after you list the property but before the property is available for showing. Thus, when the seller agrees they want staging services, there is a high probability you have captured the listing.

If you feel uncomfortable handling these suggestions directly with the seller, many interior designers provide staging services. Whether you hire a designer or help the seller yourself, the tips below will assist you in doing a better job of staging your listings.

1. *Curb appeal*

   Take the seller outside their property. Ask them to walk up to the front door just as a buyer would. What do they notice? Is the property attractive from the street? Is the lawn neatly manicured? If the weather is warm, are flowers blooming in the flowerbeds? Does the house look well maintained from the street? Is there a car parked in the driveway or worse, in the front yard? To achieve the maximum price possible for the property, the seller must address these curb appeal issues. Upgrading the landscaping, repairing any damage visible from the street, painting the trim, and parking the cars in the garage or on the street can dramatically increase how many people view the property. Remind the seller you want to motivate people to pick up the phone and schedule a showing. If a property looks run down, fewer buyers will be motivated to see it. Less exposure usually translates into a lower price.

2. *Welcoming and inviting*

   When buyers walk up to the front door, what do they notice? Does the doorbell work? What about the welcome mat? If it looks ratty, have the seller buy a new one. Does the front door need painting or re-staining? If so, repairing these items can yield a significant return. Ideally, the home should beckon the buyer to walk in and view it.

3. *Clean is a necessity*

   Few people are willing to tolerate a dirty house. Granted there are buyers who love fixers or who actively search for probates, but most buyers prefer squeaky-clean properties. If the sellers are unwilling to clean up their property, ask if they are willing to take a ten percent reduction in their sales price. This question normally captures their attention. Dirty, cluttered properties do not command the same price as pride of ownership. Be sure to have the windows and screens cleaned, all junk removed from the closets and the garage, and any unnecessary clothes or other unused items placed in storage. If the sellers do not have the time, suggest a cleaning service. It is also advisable to locate a company that removes junk from properties. This can be very handy if the seller leaves their rubbish for the buyer to cleanup.

4. *Love me—love my pet*
Fluffy may be adorable, but the best place for Fluffy may be away from the home while it is on the market. The primary reason to remove pets is to protect them. It is a nightmare if a pet disappears or is hurt because it escaped during a showing. Worse yet, if the pet harms a potential buyer, the seller could be liable for serious damages. Encourage the sellers to protect their animals by keeping them elsewhere.

Another reason to remove pets is the odor. While the owners may not be aware of the pet smell, visitors are. Like smoking odors, pet smells can be particularly difficult to remove. If the sellers are unable or unwilling to board their animals, recommend that they purchase a quality air purifier. This will eliminate a large portion of the odors. When all else fails, a plug-in air freshener can sometimes mask the smells. Regardless of whether the sellers board their pets, have them clean the carpets, the drapes, furniture, as well as any surfaces where the pet normally spends time. Thorough cleaning also helps to eliminate lingering smoke odors as well. Once the house is clean, keep the pets and smokers outside if possible.

5. *Less is more*
Homes crammed with furniture, walls covered with family photos, or cluttered counter tops all convey the same message: "This is my home filled with my possessions." This makes it particularly difficult for the buyer to imagine their belongings in the property. If the buyers cannot picture themselves living in the property, there is a high probability they will continue to search elsewhere.

To assist the seller in removing these items, tell them the truth, i.e., "To obtain the highest price possible for your property, the buyer will need to picture your property as their home." This means removing as many personal mementos as possible. Cluttered properties seldom bring as high a price as properties that look spacious and organized. Have the sellers clean the house thoroughly and simplify the décor. They will have to do this eventually—why not do it when it can help them achieve a higher purchase price?

6. *Fix it!*

   Repair anything that is broken or not functioning properly. Buyers make snap decisions about property condition. While the house may be structurally sound and all major systems working properly, unpainted trim, a leaky faucet, or an inoperable doorbell can give the impression that the property is in poor condition. To give the best impression possible, replace damaged screens and gutters and re-caulk where needed. Remember, a poor impression results in a lower sales price.

7. *Corral the kids*

   While you can't ask the sellers to board the children, make sure the children's toys are put away. If the seller is short on space, you may want to loan the seller some large plastic storage boxes to store toys during the listing period. Store the boxes in the garage during showings. Toys can be dangerous, especially for adults who wear bifocals and cannot see the floor clearly.

8. *Common "scents"*

   Odors have a strong effect on all humans. A research study testing perfume scents used cinnamon rolls as for comparison. The men in the study overwhelmingly preferred the scent of cinnamon rolls over all perfumes in the study. To create the "cinnamon roll effect," purchase canned cinnamon rolls and bake them prior to open houses or major showings. If the home has a fireplace, light a fire and use pine potpourri to accentuate the smell of burning wood.

9. *Light and bright*

   Most people prefer bright houses. If the trees have blocked the light, urge the seller to have them trimmed prior to listing the property. During showings, remember to open all drapes and to turn on all lights. To increase brightness, make sure the seller has the windows and skylights cleaned. Also, remember to have all chandeliers cleaned as well as dusting the light bulbs.

10. *Disguise what is ugly*

    Sometimes a major room faces an ugly view or the building next door. To change this, a simple white lattice and a few strategically placed plants can change ugly to beautiful. If the seller's furniture is an eyesore, suggest they purchase some slipcovers to give it a fresh look. Another alternative is to drape several attractive throws over the furniture and then add pillows on top of the throws. One important caveat here—you must disclose any structural damage in writing to all potential buyers. Concealing the truth can cost you and the seller thousands of dollars.

11. *Give weird colors the brush*

    Time after time, properties with strange colored rugs and/or walls will sit on the market until the seller decides to paint and re-carpet. If the sellers cannot afford to repaint or re-carpet the entire house, at least have them upgrade the primary rooms, i.e., the primary living area, master bedroom, and kitchen. A slightly different approach is to use computer software from some of the paint companies to repaint the room on your computer. Print out the changes and let potential buyers see what the property looks like once the computer repaints it in their colors.

12. *Create sex appeal*

    A new bedspread and plenty of pillows make the bedroom look more inviting. Strategically placed candles, different varieties of attractively packaged bubble bath, and beautifully arranged towels can spiff up a tired bath.

13. *Hire a professional decorator or stager*

Many decorators now provide staging services since it is an excellent way to obtain new business. The seller can hire a decorator for one or two hours to make suggestions about furniture placement, how to accent the home using the seller's existing possessions, as well as inexpensive ways to improve the over all appearance. To locate a good decorator, visit model homes to determine whom does quality work in your area.

Feng Shui: the Ultimate Staging Strategy

Most houses can benefit from being polished up a bit. While staging can be effective, many people believe Feng Shui produces even better results. Feng Shui is a powerful tool to differentiate yourself from the competition. In fact, approximately 20 percent of all buyers and sellers in Beverly Hills now invite a Feng Shui expert in to assist them in either preparing their home for sale or selecting the right home to purchase. While some people may consider this superstitious, thousands swear by the results. Feng Shui can be a powerful customer service tool to attract sellers and send competitors packing.

Feng Shui is an ancient Chinese belief system based upon earth signs to determine areas prone to flooding or subject to damaging winds. Feng Shui strives to create balance in both our personal and professional environments by balancing the five elements: wood, fire, earth, metal, and water. Feng Shui experts also consider how "Chi" (energy) moves in a home based on a variety of factors. Whether your sellers believe in Feng Shui or not, using the principles below will enhance the appearance of the seller's property and make it more attractive to buyers.

Ten Strategies to Create a Fortunate Environment

Feng Shui experts evaluate a variety of factors, many of which you can change. The tips below will assist you and your sellers in creating a home that invites good fortune.

1. Good exposure to sunlight is highly desirable. If trees and shrubs are overgrown, trim them away from the structure. Any plants that block the walkway to the front door should also be trimmed.

2. Are the trees and shrubs around the home healthy? Healthy plants and trees are part of the constructive or building part of the Feng Shui cycle that attracts abundance and positive outcomes. In contrast, dead landscaping represents the destructive cycle that creates poor luck and poor outcomes. Remove dead plants and replace them with healthy ones.

3. If there has been a negative event in the property (divorce, business loss, serious illness), Feng Shui experts believe you can dissipate the negative energy by smudging (burning sage and waving the smoke through each corner of each room in the house.) If burning sage makes you feel uncomfortable, you can purchase liquid smudge instead.

4. Water represents money. Drippy faucets and leaky toilets represent money dripping away. Have these items repaired. Feng Shui experts also recommend putting the lid down on the toilet and closing bathroom doors. In contrast, fountains or waterfalls that flow toward a property represent money flowing toward you. Placing a fountain near the front door is particularly auspicious in terms of attracting wealth. Advise the sellers to keep the water fresh at all times.

5. If the stairwell is visible from the front door, Feng Shui experts believe money can run away easily. To prevent the sellers from losing money, have them place a beautiful area rug in the entry. If there is room, a small table with fresh cut flowers in the center of

the rug also works. Another strategy is to hang a crystal chandelier and to place live plants adjacent to the stairs. In each case, this breaks up the energy so the money will stay inside the home.

6. Feng Shui experts believe the front door to the property is the mouth through which riches flow. To attract more riches, make the entry to the home as appealing as possible. A curved walkway to the front door is very favorable. Sellers can attract qualified buyers (i.e., prosperity and fortune) by planting or by placing pots of colorful flowers by the front door. Nothing on the front porch should block the main door nor should there be anything sharp, straight, or angular aimed at the front door. The doorbell should work (you cannot attract abundance if you don't know the bell is ringing). Make sure the doormat is in excellent condition as well. It is especially important to choose one that says, "Welcome!" In addition, place symbols of affluence such as coins, bells, or wind chimes (with hollow rods in groups of six, seven, or eight) near the front door.

7. Green and red attract money. Green is the color of money and red is associated with abundance and good luck. A simple way to add more green is with live plants. Place coins in a red sack to attract more money. To determine where to place the coins, stand in the doorway to the room. The far left hand corner is where to place the coins.

8. Feng Shui experts believe "poison arrows" may keep properties from selling. Poison arrows occur when there is too much energy directed to a single spot. For example, a house located on a "T" intersection or at the end of a cul de sac will have too much energy flowing toward it. If your seller owns this type of property, they can disperse the energy by building a fence or planting a hedge in the front of the property.

9. For sellers who have a home office, red and green are very favorable. If possible, position the desk so the person faces the door when seated. Again, adding live plants, a fountain, and coins

in a red sack placed in the far left corner will increase the flow of abundance.

10. Pay attention to intention. To make Feng Shui work for you and your sellers, examine your intention. Feng Shui relies on the energy that supports our actions. For example, providing Feng Shui services strictly to help you obtain a commission will not have the same results as when your goal is to serve others. Giving back is an important way to attract more and better things to us.

Staging services are an excellent way to differentiate your services from those of your competitors. Once you finish your action plan for Chapter 12, go to Chapter 13 to learn one of the most powerful strategies for overcoming the Big Lie.

Balance the Yin and the Yang
Shawne Mitchell, Village Realtors
Montecito, California

I have written two books on how Feng Shui affects homeowners as well as a regular column for a national magazine. As a result, many sellers and buyers hire me because of their interest in how the energy of a property affects its profit.

Whether or not the sellers believe in Feng Shui, almost everyone wants to sell their property quickly. Many houses benefit from removing the clutter and rearranging the furniture and accessories. One of the most important things that I do for my sellers is to balance the energy in the house. The ideal balance is 60 percent Yang (considered male energy) and 40 percent Yin (considered female energy.) The Yang energy includes sharp lines, hard surfaces, and plenty of light. Yang energy is considered to be stimulating. It is action or movement energy. In contrast, Yin energy is cushy, soft, dark, nurturing, gentle, and restful. Feng Shui experts believe a house with proper balance will attract a well-qualified buyer more quickly.

For example, I listed a cottage that had too much Yin energy. The property was filled with quilts, pillows, ruffles, and oval picture frames. Rugs covered most of the beautiful hardwood floors. The seller had quite a few showings but no offers. A few women liked the property, but none of the men liked it. From a Feng Shui perspective, the energy was too passive. The house lacked action energy. Even though the market was quite active, the property was listed with another agent for six months and did not sell.

When the listing expired, the seller invited me to discuss what would have to be done to make the property sell. When a house has too much Yin, the owners may not maintain it. They mean to do the repairs, but they never seem to get around to it. This was certainly true in this case. The first step was to handle the deferred maintenance. Next, we removed most of the rugs, the ruffles, and the oval picture frames. We also removed quite a bit of the clutter. When we put the property back on the market and increased the commission to six percent, the property only took three weeks to sell even though it was the slowest month of the year.

In another case, I had a man who owned a contemporary townhouse. He purchased the property new. His décor was vanilla on vanilla—light beige walls, light beige carpet, light hardwood floors, and light beige furniture. The accents were all chrome and glass. Since he worked from home, his house was packed with computers, televisions, and other electronics. The equipment and the décor made the house too masculine. To make it more balanced, we painted some of the walls maroon, taupe, and chocolate. We added dark pillows to the couch and used rugs to add more color to the floors. Once the changes were complete, it only took us two weeks to sell the property.

My clients pay me a full commission because I help them do the work necessary to sell their homes more quickly. As buyers, they also have my eye helping them to avoid properties that will be difficult to sell in the future. Because the seller pays the commission, my services cost them nothing when they are purchasing. Perhaps they really ought to be paying me for that additional service!

Chapter 12 Supporting Scripts

Sellers who stage their home can net thousands of dollars of additional profit. When a property is jam-packed with too much of everything or if the seller thinks their home is perfect the way it is, the agent must be careful about how they approach the situation. An excellent strategy for handling this discussion is to advise the sellers to protect their precious belongings prior to listing their property. They will have to pack when they move, so getting a head start is a smart idea. In addition, this will decrease the likelihood that a potential buyer might inadvertently damage something the seller treasures. A different approach is to take sellers to see model homes. Ask the sellers to note how the decorators prepared the homes for sale and assist them in achieving a similar effect in their home. A third option is to hire a decorator or a staging specialist.

Sellers who are open to Feng Shui often find they enjoy making the changes that will increase their abundance. To incorporate staging or Feng Shui services into your listing consultation, use any of the following scripts:

Script #1: Seller is open to staging their home
Making your home as attractive as possible to potential buyers can result in a substantial increase in the amount you will receive for your property. There are three ways to achieve this goal. First, you can use the simple guidelines in this handout. A second way is to hire a decorator who assists sellers in staging their homes. A third way is look at how model homes are staged and then make the appropriate changes. I'm happy to assist you with suggestions as well. Which of these strategies for staging is the most attractive to you?

Script #2: Seller is not open to staging their home
Staging your home will help you obtain the highest price possible for your property. Choosing not to stage your home can result in receiving substantially less money. The choice is yours, what would you like to do—stage your home or receive less money?

Script #3: Seller is open to using Feng Shui
Many sellers believe that using the principles of Feng Shui helps them to attract a higher quality buyer and a higher price. There are two ways to

do this. First, you can follow the Feng Shui guidelines in this handout. The other alternative is to hire a Feng Shui expert. I would be happy to make a referral. Is using Feng Shui to attract better buyers and more money a service you want?

Chapter 12 Action Plan

Pride of ownership properties command the highest prices. Staging the seller's home so it looks as attractive as possible increases the probability the seller will obtain the highest price possible in the shortest time. Remember to place a plus (+) next to each item you plan to implement in your business and place them in priority order. Leave the other items blank. Rewrite any action steps that need alteration. See Appendix A for additional resources.

Action Steps

____ 1. I will give sellers a list of suggestions to help them make their property more attractive to buyers.

____ 2. I will personally assist sellers in staging their property and offer this service during my listing consultation.

____ 3. I will locate a professional decorator who is willing to assist sellers in presenting their properties to best advantage.

____ 4. As part of my listing consultation, I will provide sellers with a list of Feng Shui tips to help them sell their home more quickly.

____ 5. I will refer sellers to a Feng Shui specialist to assist them in staging their home for a quick sale.

Assisting willing sellers in staging their property is an excellent way to build rapport and provide outstanding customer service. One of the most persuasive ways to win the seller, however, is to show them how working with you will net them more money.

Chapter 13
Overcoming the Big Lie—
Do the Numbers

Opportunity is missed by most people because it comes dressed in overalls and looks like work.
— Thomas A. Edison

What I do now and what I will add to my business:

Put a checkmark (√) next to what you do now. Leave the remaining items blank. Review the action steps at the end of the chapter to determine the strategies you will implement in your business.

____ 1. My company currently has the top list-to-sell price ratio.

____ 2. My personal list-to-sell price ratio is better than any of my competitors.

____ 3. During my listing consultation, I explain how full service brokerage assists the seller in obtaining more money for their property.

Gather Your Ammunition

"Doing the numbers" is one of the most powerful pieces of ammunition in your arsenal. The strategy below is particularly powerful, provided your company prices their listings correctly and sells them close to asking price. If this is not the case and you are a strong negotiator, use your personal data rather than your firm's data. The material below will take a little time to calculate, but it is definitely worth the effort. When you can objectively show the seller how much they will net after paying commissions, the numbers overcome the discount objection effortlessly. Once you have mastered this process, you will be amazed at how basing your listing consultation on actual sales data melts away most objections.

To use this strategy, begin by comparing "List-to-sell ratios" and calculate how much the seller will receive after deducting commission.

After determining what the seller will net if they list with your company, repeat the process for each of your competitors. Display the results as illustrated in Table 6. Print out this data and use it whenever you go on a listing consultation.

Calculate the Seller's Proceeds

To determine how much the seller will receive after deducting commissions, follow the process below.

1. From the MLS, add together the list prices for each property your firm has sold in the area during the last six months. (You can do this for your personal listings as well.) Use initial list prices rather than any price reductions. This will give you the **total volume listed**.

2. Repeat the process, except add together the closed sales price for each listing your company sold during the last six months. This will give you the **total volume sold.**

3. Divide **total volume sold** by the **total volume listed** to calculate the **selling percentage rate**.

   <u>Total volume sold</u>   = Selling percentage rate
   Total volume listed

4. Multiply the **list price** of the seller's property by the **selling percentage rate.** This equals how much the seller will net *before* paying commissions.

   Seller's list price
   x <u>**Selling percentage rate**</u>
   Seller's proceeds *before* **commissions**

5. To determine the **seller's proceeds** *after* **commissions**, calculate your six percent commission and subtract it from the seller's proceeds *before* commissions.

Seller's proceeds *before* **commissions**
– Six percent commission
Seller's proceeds *after* **commissions**

(Please note: the seller's net profit is calculated by subtracting the commission, the balance of the closing costs, and any existing loan balances.)

6. The final step compares the seller's proceeds *after* commissions to see which company nets the seller the most money.

EXAMPLE:

List price: $200,000

Your commission rate = 6%

1. Total volume listed by your firm = $6,765,000

2. Total volume sold by your firm = $6,595,000

3. Divide total volume sold by the total volume listed to calculate the selling percentage rate.

$$\frac{\$6,595,900}{\$6,765,000} = \text{Selling percentage rate} = .975$$

4. Multiply the list price by the selling percentage rate.

List Price = $200,000
Selling percentage = .975

$200,000
x_____.975
$195,000 = seller's proceeds *before* commissions

5. To find the seller's proceeds *after* commissions, subtract your six percent commission. ($195,000 x .06 = $11,700)

$195,000
– $11,700
$183,300 = Seller's proceeds *after* commissions

6. Repeat steps 1-5 for each of your competitors.

Competitor A:
Traditional Realty Firm, 5% Commission

1. Total volume listed by Competitor A = $5,364,800

2. Total volume sold by Competitor A = $5,139,600

3. Divide total volume sold by the total volume listed to calculate the selling percentage rate.

$$\frac{\$5,139,600}{\$5,364,800} = \text{Selling percentage rate} = .958$$

4. Multiply the list price by the selling percentage rate.

List Price = $200,000
Selling percentage = .958

$$\begin{array}{r} \$200,000 \\ \times \underline{\quad .958} \\ \$191,600 \end{array} = \text{seller's proceeds } \textit{before} \text{ commissions}$$

5. To find the seller's proceeds *after* commissions, subtract the five percent commission. ($191,600 x .05 = $9,580)

$$\begin{array}{r} \$191,600 \\ - \underline{\quad \$9,580} \\ \$182,020 \end{array} = \text{Competitor A seller's proceeds } \textit{after} \text{ commissions}$$

6. Compare seller's proceeds for your firm vs. Competitor A:

Your sellers receive	$183,300
Competitor A's sellers receive	−$182,020
	$1,280

Your firm nets the seller $1,280 more.

Competitor B:
On-line Discounter, 4% Listing Fee
Brokerage Lists on MLS Using VOW

1. Total volume listed = $4,232,500

2. Total volume sold = $4,003,900

3. Divide total volume sold by the total volume listed to calculate the selling percentage rate.

$\dfrac{\$4,003,900}{\$4,232,500}$ = selling percentage rate = .946

4. Multiply the list price by the selling percentage rate.

List Price = $200,000
Selling percentage = .946

$200,000
x ____.946
$189,200 = seller's proceeds *before* commissions

5. To find the seller's proceeds *after* commissions, subtract the four percent commission. ($189,200 x .04 = $7,568)

$189,200
− __$7,568
$181,632 = Competitor B seller's proceeds *after* commissions

6. Compare seller's proceeds for your firm vs. Competitor B:

Your sellers receive $183,300
Competitor B's sellers receive = $181,632
$1,668

Your firm nets the seller $1,668 more.

Competitor C:
For-Sale-by-Owner Site, 2% Commission
Includes Negotiation and Multiple Listing Service

1. Total volume listed = $1,382,500

2. Total volume sold = $1,260,000

3. Divide total volume sold by the total volume listed to calculate the selling percentage rate.

    $$\frac{\$1,260,000}{\$1,382,500} = \text{selling percentage rate} = .911$$

4. Multiply the list price by the selling percentage rate.

    Sales Price = $200,000
    Selling percentage = .911

    $200,000
    x____.911
    $182,200 = seller's proceeds *before* commissions

5. To find the seller's proceeds *after* commissions, subtract the two percent commission. ($182,200 x .02 = $3,644)

    $182,200
    − $3,644
    $178,556 = Competitor C seller's proceeds *after* commissions

6. Compare the seller's net for your firm vs. Competitor C:

Your sellers receive	$183,300
Competitor C's sellers receive	− $178,556
	$4,744

    Your firm nets the seller $4,744 more

    Create a flyer for your listing consultation like the one in Table 6.
    174

Table 6: Sample Listing Consultation Flyer

Put More Money in Your Pocket!

Our Company
List Price	$200,000
Selling percentage rate	x .975
Seller proceeds *before* commissions	$195,000
Less 6% commission	− $11,700
Seller proceeds *after* commissions	**$183,300**

Five Percent Competitor
List Price	$200,000
Selling percentage rate	x .958
Seller proceeds *before* commissions	$191,600
Less 5% commission	− $9,580
Seller proceeds *after* commissions	**$182,020**

My Company Nets You $1,280 MORE

Four Percent On-line Broker
List Price	$200,000
Selling percentage rate	x .946
Seller proceeds *before* commissions	$189,200
Less 4% commission	− $7,568
Seller proceeds *after* commissions	**$181,632**

My Company Nets You $1,668 MORE

Two Percent For-Sale-by-Owner Broker
List Price	$200,000
Selling percentage rate	x .911
Seller proceeds *before* commissions	$182,200
Less 2% commission	− $3,784
Seller Proceeds *after* commissions	**$178,416**

My Company Nets You $4,884 MORE

Best Price AND Best Service—Can You Afford Anything Less?

Very few things are as persuasive as a clear presentation of market statistics. Like any type of math, the first few times you use the formulas may be challenging. With regular use, however, it will become second nature.

Once you finish determining which steps you will take on the Action Plan, go to Chapter 14 to learn how risk management strategies can provide you with a powerful way to overcome the competition.

Show Them the Expireds

Tim Burrell, RE/MAX Palos Verdes, California,
and Prudential Carolinas Realty
Raleigh, North Carolina

Technology and two great teams make it possible for me to sell real estate in California and North Carolina. The difference in the two markets is striking. California is still in a raging sellers' market, although it has slowed down somewhat. Now we're only receiving two offers rather than fifteen on our listings. It is also very litigious. In contrast, Raleigh has been in strong buyers' market since the dot-com crash. Approximately twenty percent of all transactions in Southern California fall apart. In Raleigh, we have had only five transactions cancel out of the last three hundred we have sold.

For us, the customer is more important than we are. When we take a listing, we do more than just provide a virtual tour or high quality brochure. To show our listings to best advantage, we have our technology specialist who shoots and edits our virtual tours. We also edit all brochure photos in Photoshop to improve the quality of the image presentation. In terms of technology, we use Top Producer on-line, eFrogg, and Settlement Room for transaction management. For lead generation, we use e-Agent.biz, Keynames.com and RealProSystems.com. The key ingredient is having good people on both coasts.

Since I do most of the listing presentations, I'm usually the one who fields the discount objections. The three key points I stress during my listing presentation are:

1. We will get your property sold rather than having it expire.

2. We will help you obtain more money for your property.

3. Your sale will be more secure.

Many sellers in California mistakenly believe they can obtain a great price by discounting or selling themselves. What they don't realize is the red-hot market does not allow buyers' agents the luxury of showing buyers all the properties prior to writing an offer. When the buyers find a property they like, they must write it up immediately or it will be sold in multiple offers. In Raleigh, sellers need additional services because there are too many listings and not enough buyers. The result is discounted listings often expire. In fact, one of the easiest ways to overcome the discount objection is to print out a list of the expired listings. In both areas, the overwhelming majority of expireds are listed with discounters. After showing the seller the MLS printouts I ask,

> *How much will you save when the discount broker does not sell your house? You only pay the Realtor® when you sell your house, right? When your house does not sell, the amount of commission is irrelevant.*

A second strategy is to show the seller how you help them obtain more money for their property. I do this by constructing a spreadsheet and showing it to the sellers on my laptop. My current list-to-sell price ratio in California is 108 percent. When I compare it to the discounters in our market, their list-to-sell price ratio is in the 90 to 98 percent range. This means on average, sellers can make up to 18 percent more when they list with us. This dwarfs the small amount the seller would save by discounting the commission.

The third strategy is to secure the sale. Because I'm a licensed attorney in California, I am very aggressive about securing the sale on both sides of the transaction. Sellers often grouse about all the required disclosures in California. I explain to them that these disclosures protect them from problems after the sale closes and then ask,

"Do you want to stand behind your lawyer or do you want to be on your own?" On the buyer's side, I personally contact the lenders and cross-examine them by asking:

1. *Have you run the buyer's credit?*

2. *Are you willing to state in writing that these buyers will definitely be able to obtain their loan?*

3. *Does this sale depend upon the sale of another house?*

4. *Is there anything else that will come up during the course of this sale that I should know now?*

To work with us, clients must qualify. Rather than concealing problems, we explain how our excellent team of real estate professionals, inspectors, lenders, and other top-notch service providers can help our clients resolve almost any problem. All we need is the whole truth. When we sense clients are trying to hide-the-ball, we refuse to do business with them. We sometimes miss a few transactions, but we avoid a tremendous amount of heartache and trouble.

Chapter 13 Supporting Scripts

In many cases, strong agents will find their list-to-sell price ratios will be substantially higher than those ratios for their company. To improve your list-to-sell price ratio, you must be able to persuade your sellers to be realistic about their asking price. Taking even one overpriced listing can ruin your competitive advantage in this area.

To avoid overpricing your listings, remind the sellers that approximately 95 percent of all properties involve a loan. This means the lender's appraisal must support the purchase price the buyers are willing to pay. When appraisals come in low, the transaction generally falls apart. Remember, the lender will base the appraisal upon closed prices, not on list prices.

Most agents are familiar with the "honeymoon chart" that shows most showings take place during the first 30 days a property is on the market. Sellers who sell during the honeymoon period usually receive more money for their property than sellers who take longer to sell. This is due to the backlog of buyers who are currently looking and have yet to find a property. After this initial rush, showings drop substantially because the bulk of the active buyers saw it when it first came on the market. To implement the list-to-sell ratios into your listing consultation, use any of the scripts below. Additional scripts for using this strategy are contained in Chapter 18.

Script #1: Agent has best list-to-sell ratio
As you can see from this chart, sellers who list with me actually receive a higher net amount from the sale of their property than they do from listing with other companies that offer a lower commission. Is netting the maximum amount from your sale a service you want?

Script #2: Agent has best list-to-sell ratio and seller still asks for a discount
As you can see from this chart, sellers who list with me actually receive a higher net amount from the sale of their property than they do from listing with other companies that offer a lower commission. Consequently, you have an important decision to make. You can list with me and net the highest possible amount from your property or you can list with someone

else who will charge you less commission and may net your less. The choice is yours, what would you like to do?

Script #3: Agent does not have best list-to-sell ratio among traditional competitors, but has a better ratio than discount competitors have

As you can see from this chart, the companies who represent sellers for a reduced commission do not net as much as those sellers represented by my company. Consequently, you have an important decision to make. Do you want to focus exclusively on commission or do you want to net the highest possible amount from the sale of your property? It's your choice. What would you like to do?

Using your own version of the handout in Table 6 is a powerful way to illustrate the benefits of listing at a full commission.

Chapter 13 Action Plan

In most cases, it is easier for an individual agent to develop a higher list-to-sell ratio than it is for a company. While this may seem daunting, remember it's simply a matter of pricing your listings correctly. See Resources for additional help in this area.

To implement the list-to-sell price ratios in your listing presentation, follow the action steps below. Remember to place a plus (+) next to each item you plan to implement in your business and place them in priority order. Leave the other items blank. Rewrite any action steps that need alteration.

Action Steps

____ 1. I will evaluate my company and my personal list-to-sell price ratio to determine which one is better.

____ 2. I will compare our list-to-sell ratios with those of competitors to determine if I can use this in my listing consultations.

____ 3. If a competitor has a better list-to-sell ratio than I do, I will work on improving my listing consultation pricing dialogue until my list-to-sell ratio is better than that of my competitors.

____ 4. During my listing consultation, I will explain how full service brokerage assists the seller in obtaining more money for their property.

____ 5. For each of my listing consultations, I will prepare a chart like the one in Table 6 that shows how my services help the seller net the highest possible price for their property.

While the numbers above indicate what happens on the front end of the transaction, few agents discuss the other places where the seller can lose tens of thousands of dollars. The next weapon is one most agents never consider using. Given today's highly litigious environment, a strong risk management strategy may be an excellent way to defeat the competition while providing an important defense for your seller.

Chapter 14
Uncover Your Opponent's Hidden Weaknesses: What Your Competitor Fails to Disclose Leaves the Seller Exposed

We are continually faced by great opportunities brilliantly disguised as insoluble problems.
—Lee Iacocca

What I do now and what I will add to my business:

Put a checkmark (√) next to what you do now. Leave the remaining items blank. Review the action steps at the end of the chapter to determine the strategies you will implement in your business.

_____ 1. My company has a risk management program.

_____ 2. I discuss risk management issues as part of my listing consultation.

_____ 3. I take specific steps to ensure the sellers make all required disclosures.

Avoid Litigation Minefields

The two most common reasons for real estate litigation are failure to disclose and agency violations. When real estate agents fail to listen and respond to the consumer's wants and needs, lawsuits result. Surprisingly, few agents incorporate a risk management discussion in their listing consultations. Part of the challenge is persuading the seller to be completely forthcoming with respect to all disclosure items. Failure to address disclosure issues, however, can expose all parties to costly litigation. To distinguish yourself from risky competitors, include a discussion of risk management strategies in your Waging War listing consultation. Not only does effective risk management distinguish you from the competition, it protects the seller from potential litigation.

Since disclosure requirements vary from state to state, check with your broker or local board to determine the exact disclosure requirements in your area.

Ten Guidelines to Keep You Out of Trouble

The discussion below provides general suggestions that can limit exposure to litigation. A separate list of sellers' issues will follow this section, including strategies for incorporating these issues into your Waging War listing consultation.

1. Understand Your Disclosure Obligations

What does your state require in terms of disclosure? What are your responsibilities? What obligations do the buyer and seller have with respect to the disclosure process? For example, is the seller required to give the buyer a written disclosure statement prior to seeing an offer? Who is responsible for delivering the disclosure statement to the buyer? How long does the buyer have to disapprove an item? If the buyer disapproves an item, may the seller cancel the transaction and accept a back-up offer? What properties are exempt from the state disclosure laws? How do you handle deaths on the property, including deaths from a violent crime or AIDS? If the seller or buyer refuses to fill out the disclosures in a timely fashion, what are your obligations? In addition to state and federal disclosure requirements, what are the local requirements? What remedies are available to the buyer if the seller misrepresents the property? If you cannot answer each of these questions, you are putting yourself and your clients at risk.

a. Listing agent's disclosure obligations

Most states require listing and selling agents to conduct an independent investigation of the property, even when the seller and/or buyer provide an inspection report. In addition to requiring a visual inspection, most states also require listing agents to make an inquiry of the seller. This means that the listing agent must ask the seller about any reports in their possession, about any work the seller has completed during the time they owned the property, as well as about any other conditions that could materially affect the desirability of the property. Even when the agent conducts a seller inquiry, it is still unwise to rely solely on the seller's representations or on an inspector's report.

b. *Buyer agent's disclosure obligations*

Most states also require the buyer's agent to conduct an independent inspection of the property no matter what the sellers and buyers decide to do. If the seller provides the buyers with any reports, insist that the buyers hire their own specialists to verify the accuracy of the reports. If they refuse to do so, send them a letter advising them to seek an independent inspection. If they still refuse, have them sign a hold harmless agreement to protect you and your firm. (Your company's legal staff must draft any "hold harmless" agreement.)

2. Disclose—Don't Diagnose!

Agents often enjoy being the expert. This is a great way to end up in big trouble. For example, when a buyer asks about the brown stain on the ceiling, many agents will assume there is a roof leak. A better way to handle this situation is to tell the buyer,

> *The best way to determine the cause of the problem is to have a thorough physical inspection of the property.*

Furthermore, on your disclosure statement you would note, "Brown stain noted on powder room ceiling."

Brown stains can be water leaks, but brown stains can also result from a beehive in the attic. Remember, AVOID DIAGNOSING. Instead, note what you see but avoid stating the cause. Here are some additional examples:

a. "Roof leak noted on ceiling" vs. "brown stain noted on ceiling."

b. "Deck has separated from the house due to settling" vs. "Separation noted between deck and house."

c. "Mildew stains noted on shower" vs. "black substance noted on shower."

d. "Asbestos noted on gravity heating system" vs. "white flaky substance noted on heating ducts."

e. "Sidewalk damage noted due to tree roots" vs. "sidewalk damage noted adjacent to tree."

Avoid analyzing, diagnosing, or explaining defects. Even if you are an expert, let the licensed/bonded professionals evaluate the nature of the problem. If the buyer or seller asks your opinion, use the language below when you respond:

If you are concerned about this problem, the wisest course of action is to seek an independent inspection of each item.

Be sure to document the conversation in writing and place it in your transaction file. Being this precise about how you speak to buyers and sellers may seem like splitting hairs. If you ever face a hostile attorney during a deposition, however, you will quickly learn that what you say and how you say it is extremely important. In the tree root example above, an attorney badgered the agent who "diagnosed" the problem for not knowing whether the damage resulted from the trees, from an earthquake, or from a broken pipe. Remember, disclose but do NOT diagnose!

3. If Your State Requires You to Inspect the Property, Be Thorough

Use an inspection strategy that enables you to avoid missing any areas inside or outside the property when you do your agent's inspection. The "right wall inspection" strategy described below works well to minimize potential problems.

a. Walk up to the property. Notice the sidewalks, yard, and hard surfaces. Now, walk to your right and walk the entire property. Note any damage or any other "red flag" you may observe.

Make special note of cracking, trip hazards, and any signs of slippage or drainage problems.

b. When you return to the front of the property, repeat the process by walking around all structures on the property.

c. To do an interior inspection, walk through the front door and follow the right wall throughout the house. As you look at each wall, look from floor to ceiling along the wall. Note stains, cracking, and any other types of damage. Notice whether the doors are plumb in the doorframe.

d. Remember, most states do NOT require you to do any of the following:
   1. Look in areas that are not visibly accessible, such as on top of the roof or under the house.
   2. Flush toilets, turn on the stove, open cabinets, open windows, etc.
   3. Diagnose or state the cause of any items you observe.

4. "I Don't Know" is Often Your Best Answer

Saying, "I don't know," may seem contradictory to providing the seller with excellent service. The examples below from actual lawsuits illustrate why "I don't know" is often the best thing you can say.

Scenario #1:

Listing agent obtains a listing on a new house. The builder/seller informs the listing agent that the property is 4,500 square feet and shows the agent the plans. Based upon these representations, the listing agent lists the size of the improvements as being 4,500 square feet in the MLS. When prospective buyers look at the property, the listing agent informs them that the square footage of the improvements is 4,500 square feet.

Outcome:

The improvements were only 3,500 square feet. After the transaction closed, the buyer sued the agent and the builder/seller for misrepresenting the square footage.

The Judgment:

The court ruled that the seller and the brokers misrepresented the size of the improvements. The judgment required the seller and the brokers to pay damages plus reimbursing the buyer for adding an additional 1,000 square feet of improvements. When the seller declared bankruptcy, the brokers became responsible for paying the judgment.

Smart Agent Strategy:

Advise the buyer to have a surveyor or appraiser measure the property to determine the exact lot size and square footage.

Scenario #2:

Listing Agent lists a tear down in an estate area where vacant land is selling for $100 per square foot. The lot is 22,000 square feet and completely flat. The prospective buyer asks the agent if the entire lot is buildable. The agent replies "Yes." Based upon that representation, the buyer purchases the property. When the buyer receives the preliminary title report (survey), the report reveals a utility easement that prevents the buyer from building on the front part of the property.

Outcome:

The buyer sued the broker for misrepresentation. The easement made 2,100 square feet of the lot unusable.

The Judgment:

For buyer and against broker. The broker had to reimburse buyer $210,000 for the unusable portion of the property plus attorney fees.

Smart Agent Strategy:
Advise the buyer to check with the local zoning commission as well as checking the title to determine whether the entire property is buildable.

Remember, do not rely on representations made to you by the seller or by anyone else. Avoid making representations about exact closing costs, square footage, or lot size. When asked about square footage or lot size, your best reply is,

> *I don't know the exact square footage. To be accurate, you will need to have a survey to determine the exact lot size or an appraiser to determine the exact square footage of the improvements.*

If square footage or lot size is a matter of public record, you may give the buyer/seller the public record information. Warn them, however, that public records are often incorrect and that they must obtain a survey or appraisal to determine the exact size of the lot or improvements. If the seller or listing agent makes square footage or lot size representations, advise the buyer to verify those representations with their own inspectors.

5. Disclose Old Inspection Reports

Most sellers and agents cringe at this thought. Again, determine what your state policy is in this area. Even if disclosure is not required, hiding relevant information about the property will give the buyer's attorney a field day in court. It's simply not worth the risk. Many states require sellers to disclose all reports in their possession. If a seller advises you not to make the disclosure, most states still require you to disclose any item that may materially affect the value or condition of the subject property. Furthermore, you may also have to disclose any facts you know about or conditions you observe on your diligent visual inspection of the accessible areas of the property.

In terms of the buyers, always insist that they obtain their own inspection reports. Encourage the buyers to rely on their own reports and not on those from anyone else. If you elect to give the buyer the names of inspectors, never give just one name. Always give them the name of at least three inspectors if possible. Whenever possible, only recommend inspection professionals who have adequate amounts of Errors and Omissions insurance. If buyers object to the price of the inspection, remind them that they probably pay more to insure their car annually. A thorough physical inspection can help both parties avoid thousands of dollars of costly repairs in the future. Furthermore, it is in everyone's best interest to know the condition of the property prior to purchasing.

6. Make Sure Buyers Have All Necessary Inspection Reports

Just because a piece of land is flat does not mean it is safe geologically. Radon is invisible. Many times, so are termites. To protect all parties involved, make sure the buyer orders the appropriate reports, including any hazardous materials reports. If you work in an area where there are flood zones, make sure the buyers know they will need flood insurance since their homeowner's policy does not protect them. If you live in a geologically active area, make sure the sellers require the buyers to obtain a geological report. If the buyers refuse to obtain the report, have them sign a "hold harmless" clause. Again, protect all parties involved by doing a complete job on disclosure and making sure all parties know how to take the necessary steps to protect themselves.

7. Don't Fill Out Forms for the Seller or Buyer

A company in California lost a major lawsuit because an agent dumped coffee on the disclosure statement and copied the information onto a new form. While it is great to be helpful, when it comes to disclosure, fill out only the items your state requires. Make sure the principals in the transaction complete the disclosures in their own handwriting. If not, the attorney who sues you will be sure to point it out to the judge. Worse yet, in some states, this could cost you your license.

8. Be a Conduit of Information

Never try to force a client to close a transaction if the client has concerns about disclosure items. Instead, obtain additional inspections if needed. If the buyers are still uncertain, allow them to cancel rather than buying a lawsuit. Your role is to facilitate the sale—not to decide whether or not to purchase.

9. How Long do You Need to Keep Your Files?

Technically, FOREVER! With respect to the statute of limitations, the statute in most states does not begin to run until the buyer knew or should have known of the fraud or misrepresentation. Attorneys normally allege fraud or misrepresentation when they file a "failure to disclose" lawsuit. Thus, there is no time period that effectively bars this type of claim. If your broker does not have a complete file, the Court/Department of Real Estate will look to your personal file as a backup.

10. Post-close Disclosures

Sometimes disclosure issues turn up on the day of closing or afterwards. You can often prevent post-close disclosure problems by asking the following questions:

Have you patched or repaired any interior or exterior cracks?

Are you aware of any cracking, shifting, or separation of the walls or of any other part of the property?

What repairs and maintenance have you done to the property during the time you have owned it? Was the work done to code and with a permit? *

Ask for copies of the receipts for the work as well as the permits.

Have you remodeled or made structural changes to any part of the property? If so, was the work done to code and with a permit?

* Please note: some regions do not require permits. Others require permits for any change or repair that exceeds $100. Be sure you are familiar with the policies in your area.

When you represent the buyers, encourage them to obtain reports from bonded and insured inspectors who will guarantee their inspections. Always confirm in writing that the clients have chosen their own inspection professionals. Also, remember home inspections are limited in scope. The client has the option of involving other specialists if concerned.

If a problem occurs after the transaction closes, it is critical that you continue your role of disclosing. Stay calm if you are speaking to someone who is upset. Write down what they say and repeat it back to make sure it is correct. Do not take sides. Instead, gather information and see if you can uncover what really happened. Take extensive notes throughout the process. Most importantly, consult your manager/legal advisor as soon as any problem occurs.

Just Say No to Litigation!
Craig Ashley, Prudential California Realty
Los Angeles, California

Often the best response you can give a seller who asks you to dis-count is to "Just say no!" Don't explain, don't make up excuses, and don't try to justify your commission. Sit there and wait for the seller to speak. If the seller persists, there are a number of scripts that work equally well.

If the seller is a doctor, lawyer, or CPA, I tailor my questions based upon their profession. For example, if I'm speaking to a doc-tor who needs surgery, I ask whether he would request his surgeon to discount his fee. The answer is always "No." People don't expect to obtain the best-of-the-best at a discount. At that point, all I need to do is to demonstrate we're the best team to handle their transac-tion.

When a seller has not heard of us, my standard reply is, "The best don't need to advertise." I support the services we provide with testimonials from past clients. We normally ask the sellers to com-pare our services to those provided by other agents and make the decision that is best for them.

One of my clients enjoys sparring with me over commissions. She constantly asks for concessions throughout the transaction, not just when we sign the listing or purchase agreement. Sometimes it can be something as small as $100 repair. My response is, "You have a choice. You can pay the $100 repair bill or you can back out of the deal and be sued for specific performance. What would you like to do?" She usually pays, but not without trying to get me to reduce my commission first. One of the reasons she continues to hire us is that we help her fulfill her investment goals. She likes purchasing prop-erties she can sell in two to three years with a six-figure profit. Part of earning a full commission is meeting your client's needs. When she sells, we help her obtain the highest possible price for her property. She still tries to get us to give up part of our commission, but it usually doesn't work.

While scripts are useful, it is equally important to share the realities of the market with our clients. In Southern California, litigation is a huge issue. Sellers have tremendous exposure to litigation when they choose to represent themselves or have a poorly trained agent represent them. Because of this, I remind sellers of the old adage, "You get what you pay for." Even though our company has deep pockets, we do as much as possible to avoid litigation. We are extremely careful about what we say, who does our inspections, and the disclosures we make. What amazes me is the number of agents who make statements that can get them sued. It seems like we always have to clean up messes made by careless or poorly trained agents. In fact, I have one client who has collected *two* six-figure judgments due to serious misrepresentations made by poorly trained agents. Clients often don't realize the consequences of hiring cutrate representation. It can literally cost them hundreds of thousands of dollars. One of the most important services we provide is to help our sellers "Just say no to litigation."

With some sellers, scripts and market realities do not work. If the sellers still insist on a reducing the commission, I thank them for their time and stand up to leave. It's surprising how many sellers will not let you walk out the door. In most cases, they are just testing the water. They want full service, but they want to determine if we will provide it at a reduced rate. When we're willing to "Just say no," they usually agree to list with us.

A Knock Out Risk Management Strategy

Most agents would rather have a root canal than discuss risk management strategies in detail during their listing consultation. This very fact, however, is exactly what makes using this weapon so effective. To minimize discussing this issue in detail and to keep your Waging War listing consultation moving, use the Risk Management Guide in Table 7.

Table 7

Do not use the Waging War Risk Management Guide until you have verified that all items conform to the practices your company and the law requires.

Risk Management Guide

Our company wants to minimize your exposure to costly litigation. Therefore, we strongly urge you and your listing agent to complete each of the following steps.

____ 1. Review Agency Disclosure requirements with your agent prior to signing listing agreement.

____ 2. Your listing agent should also explain what happens if your agent or another agent from our company sells the property without an outside broker (i.e., the "dual agency" requirements.)

____ 3. Please put all property defects in writing on the disclosure statement. State law requires agents to disclose any problems they observe as well. Making a complete disclosure not only limits your risk, it also decreases the probability that you will have to pay for additional repairs after your property is under contract.

____ 4. We strongly recommend giving the disclosure statement to the buyers prior to the time they write an offer. This allows the buyer to investigate any concerns they have at the beginning of the transaction. It also increases the probability your transaction will close in a timely manner

____ 5. Please give your listing agent any past inspection reports you have in your possession. Failure to do so could make you liable for failure to disclose.

____ 6. Have you made any changes to your property that may require a permit? If so, please provide your listing agent with copies of the permits. If you have made improvements without acquiring permits, please inform your agent. In some locations, your local municipality can require you to change the property back to its original condition if there is no permit for the improvements.

___ 7. We do not provide exact estimates of closing costs since this can lead to litigation. Instead, your agent will review the approximate amount of closing costs as a percentage of the purchase price. No one can precisely estimate closing costs until the transaction closes.

___ 8. If your local MLS requires agents to measure the property, they will do so. However, NEVER quote lot size or square footage information to potential buyers. If you or the agent do so, you can be liable for the differences. Instead, advise the buyer to have the property and improvements measured by a professional appraiser and/or surveyor.

___ 9. Avoid diagnosing problems. In other words, if you have a brown stain on the ceiling, avoid attributing it to a roof leak unless you are certain there is a problem with the roof. This is especially true for agents. When agents diagnose problems rather than referring the question to a qualified inspection specialist, they put you and your property at risk for litigation.

___ 10. Carefully review all federal, state, and local environmental hazard requirements with your listing agent. The law requires your agent to inquire about whether your property is near a hazardous waste dump, landfill, abandoned gas station, auto-wrecking yard, chemical plant, refinery, chemically or heavily pesticide treated agricultural land, industrial waste, etc. Agents are also required to inquire about the presence of radon, asbestos, lead-based paint, noise pollution (including noisy neighbors), etc.

Remember:
What You Fail to Disclose Can Leave You Exposed

The preceding section describes real estate disclosure strategies you must address to protect both your clients and your license. Convincing sellers to be completely honest about the condition of their property can be challenging. Often the sellers don't notice problems they have lived with for years. Occasionally, some sellers may actually cover up problems. To minimize litigation risks, encourage the seller to be proactive in making a complete and honest disclosure of the property's condition.

Managing Risk Management Disclosures

Some sellers may be reluctant to make a complete and full disclosure. They feel disclosing all problems will cost them money or prevent the sale. Surprisingly, people purchase terrible properties with major defects, provided the seller discloses these issues up front. On the other hand, when the seller hides defects and the buyers discover them later, the sale usually cancels. This can result in failure-to-disclose litigation. Even if the buyer does not litigate, the seller must still begin the marketing process over again. Furthermore, most states require the agent to disclose past inspection reports to subsequent buyers.

Sometimes sellers are aware of problems, but are not particularly concerned. For example, the sellers may not notice the sloping floors that indicate a foundation problem. When you spot this type of potential problem, do NOT diagnose. Instead, advise the sellers to note the sloping floors on their inspection disclosure. If they elect not to disclose the floor problem and your state requires you to fill out a disclosure, then avoid diagnosing. Your disclosure should simply read,

"Sloping floors noted in entry, kitchen, and dining room." If the buyer asks you to diagnose the problem, respond by saying,

Mr. and Mrs. Buyer, if you are concerned about the floors, hire an inspector to conduct an independent investigation.

If the seller knows of a problem and demands you hide it, inform your supervising broker immediately. In most cases, the smart move is to cancel the listing rather than representing someone who is pressuring you to violate the law.

A second item the sellers may find to be controversial is giving the buyer a copy of the disclosure prior to or at the time they write the offer.

If the buyer knows about the drawbacks of the property prior to writing an offer, the buyer will be less likely to ask the seller to lower the price based upon the inspections.

Permits are another area that can cause tremendous difficulty. For example, in Los Angeles County, you must obtain a permit to replace an old water heater or dishwasher. Furthermore, if the owner adds a new master bedroom and fails to obtain a permit, the city can force the owner to return the property to its original condition. Other municipalities have no permit requirements at all. To protect all parties involved, familiarize yourself with what is required in your market area as well as the potential penalties for violating the building code.

Chapter 14 Supporting Scripts

Discussing risk management and requesting full disclosure can be difficult, especially when the seller has something to hide. Because we live in a highly litigious society, having this conversation with your sellers may be the best way to protect them (and you) from costly litigation. Most sellers will appreciate your concern and will respond favorably. If the seller is hiding something, this conversation will often bring the issue to the surface. If this happens, you must decide whether you will work with a seller who may be a high risk for litigation.

In terms of differentiating your services from the competition, very few agents address risk management. This is an easy way to differentiate your services. To implement the risk management conversation in your listing consultation, use any of the scripts below. (Additional scripts are contained in Chapter 18.)

> Script #1: Company has a risk management program*
> *You may substitute your company's risk management suggestions rather than relying on the Risk Management Guide in this book.
>
> *The best way to limit your exposure to litigation is to follow the guidelines on this Risk Management Guide.*
>
> Hand them the guide and continue the conversation:

Buyers will purchase almost anything if the defects are disclosed up front. What no one likes, however, is learning about problems after the property is under contract. To avoid costly litigation, my company strongly recommends that you follow each item on the Risk Management Guide carefully. Is limiting your risk of litigation a service you want?

Script #2: Company lacks risk management program; Agent will use Risk Management Guide

The best way to limit your exposure to litigation is to follow the guidelines on this Risk Management Guide.

Hand them the Risk Management Guide and continue the conversation:

Buyers will purchase almost anything if the defects are disclosed up front. What no one likes, however, is learning about problems after the property is under contract. Following the suggestions on the Risk Ma°nagement Guide will help you avoid costly litigation. Is limiting your risk of litigation a service you want?

Script #3: Seller does not want to make a full disclosure

Did I understand correctly, that you do not want to disclose the problem with _____ to prospective buyers?

Wait for their response.

You have an important decision to make. You can make the appropriate disclosures as required by law or you can run the risk of being sued for failure to disclose. The choice is yours. What would you like to do?

If the seller is unwilling to make the disclosures required by law, walk away from the listing. It's simply too costly to take the risk of being sued.

Chapter 14 Action Plan

You may be tempted to skip the action items in this chapter. The risk management discussion is a high-level conversation that shows the seller you are an experienced professional. It's definitely worth the effort and it's easy to do when you use the Risk Management Guide.

As in previous chapters, place a plus (+) next to each item you plan to implement in your business. Rewrite any action steps that need alteration.

Action Plan

____ 1. I will discuss my company's risk management program during my next listing presentation.

____ 2. I will use the Risk Management Guide from this chapter as part of my listing consultation.

____ 3. I will take specific steps to ensure the sellers make all required disclosures.

The last 14 chapters have been devoted to laying the groundwork for your Waging War listing consultation. You are now ready to prepare your offense.

Waging War Using
Competitor Reconnaissance

*That most dangerous of opponents: the one who took
pains to comprehend the position of his adversary.*
—Piers Anthony

Chapter 15
Waging War Using
Competitor Reconnaissance

You can discover what your enemy fears most
by observing the means he uses to frighten you.
—Eric Hoffer

The Best Defense is a Good Offense

The last 14 chapters have covered a variety of ways to win the seller and defeat your competitors. What strategies will you use to win the listing? How will you differentiate your services from those provided by your competitors? Before deciding, it is important to note that the top producers interviewed in the Field Reports normally use one or two strategies coupled with strong supporting scripts. A second thing to note is their level of confidence. They know their services support the seller's goal of obtaining the highest possible net price for their property. As you look over their strategies and scripts, note how each agent articulates a strength they have as the core element of their Unique Selling Proposition (USP).

Before deciding on your personal USP, it is important to identify what services your competitors offer. Then go back to your priority list. Based upon your personal strengths and way of doing business, what services can you provide that your competitors do not provide? These two or three services will be the core pieces of your USP. These services form your first line of defense against discounters and traditional competitors.

To overcome competitors and win the consumer, you must identify how your USP differs from theirs. To achieve this objective, conduct competitor reconnaissance. Determine how quickly their listings sell, how close they sell to asking price, and how many of their listings expire and/or are listed with another broker. Once you determine what your competitors provide, you must articulate how your unique services help the seller net more money.

An important part of every listing consultation is the discussion of what all brokers do, what my company does that is different, and what I do that is different. To eliminate your rivals, provide the sellers with your list of services and then ask them to compare them to your rival's services. You will do this during your listing consultation when you discuss, "What I do that makes me different."

While it may be tempting to offer a huge list of services, this can create unrealistic expectations. A better approach is to offer less than you think you can deliver and deliver more than you promise. Nothing will harm your business more than promising the seller a host of services and not making good on those promises. Remember, offering three or four services your competitors lack may be all you need to capture the listing at a full commission.

Furthermore, if you clearly demonstrate the value of using your services in terms of the seller's bottom line, most sellers will opt for the full service approach. Let's face it, why would the seller do all the work required with most discount and limited service brokerage models if they can have full service AND a higher bottom line? When your competitor only has their discount as their primary value proposition and you provide a host of other attractive services, most sellers will opt for maximum service.

To conduct a complete investigation, begin by examining your competitors' print advertising campaigns. How much do they advertise? Do they have an 800 Call Capture service?

Next, visit your competitors' websites. Compare their web rankings with those of your company. Determine whether you will reference Alexa.com rankings as part of your consultation by comparing their web traffic with that of your company.

Carefully investigate as much information as possible about your competitors. Ask past and present clients about their experience with other firms. Identify what they liked and disliked. Determine how many of your competitors offer risk management, Call Capture, an international marketing strategy, the ability to harvest web leads, multiple open house programs, and staging services. Remember, your objective is to provide the same key services your competitors offer in addition to providing three or four services they do not offer.

How to Conduct Competitor Reconnaissance

Since very few agents thoroughly investigate their competitors' value proposition, completing the exercise below gives you a strong competitive advantage. There are six steps in the process. The steps are described below and detailed in the easy-to-use worksheets on the following pages (Tables 8-13).

Step #1: What do you currently offer?
Begin the process by identifying the items you and/or your company currently provide.

Step #2: What are you adding to your Unique Selling Proposition (USP) from the preceding chapters?
If you plan to implement additional services from the preceding chapters, note those on the worksheet as well.

Step #3: What do your competitors currently offer?
Investigate your competitors. Do this by visiting their websites to uncover the services they offer. Compare their search engine and Alexa rankings against your personal and company web rankings. Speak with clients who have considered working with your competitors. Interview agents who were affiliated with your competitors in the past. Obtain as much information as possible about their services and enter it on the worksheet.

Step #4: What services give you a competitive advantage?
Once you complete the process, your first priority is to identify specific services none of your competitors provides. These services will form the core of your personal USP when you prepare your Waging War listing consultation.

Step #5: What services give your competitors an advantage?
Identify services your competitors offer that you and/or your company do not provide. Make every effort to implement these services to stay competitive.

Step #6: What key services do your sellers want and need?

Identify 10 to 15 additional services you can offer your clients. These services will form the balance of the USP you will use in your listing consultation.

Remember, in most cases, all you need to do to win the consumer at a full commission is to offer three or four services your competitors do not provide.

Battle Plan #1
Strategic Marketing

Discounted commissions attract sellers who want to increase their bottom line. What surprises many sellers, however, is the discounter charges an increased commission when the seller wants negotiation assistance or asks to place the property on the MLS. To beat your competitors at their own game, use their "Menu of Services" approach, but provide more service. A Menu of Services is simply a list of different levels of service available at different commission rates. For example, sellers receive a reduced commission if they hold their open houses and do their own showings and negotiations. Sellers who want to have an agent handle these functions pay additional commission.

To implement this strategy in your listing consultation, use the results of your competitor reconnaissance. Begin by listing at least five things that you and/or your company provide that your competitors do not provide. Rather than discussing every service on the Competitor Reconnaissance Worksheet, focus on these five critical services your competitors do not offer (i.e., your USP) PLUS the primary services you believe the seller will want. For a sample of how this looks, see Table 14, "The Strategic Marketing Plan."

Table 8: Competitor Reconnaissance Worksheet

Part 1: Marketing to Other Agents

Services	US	C21	CB	ERA	EXT	GMA	KW	PRU	RMX	IND	DIS
1. Top list-to-sell price ratio											
2 Listing posted to local Multiple Listing Service											
3. Call agents with listings in same area & move-up areas to promote listing											
4. Call agents with buyers who work this area to promote listing											
5. E-mail brochure to agents with buyers & listing agents who work this area											
6. E-mail brochure to agents with listings in move-up areas											
7. Color brochures delivered to other brokers											

KEY:

1. US   =   Your company
2. C21 =   Century 21
3. CB   =   Coldwell Banker
4. ERA =   ERA Realty
5. EXT =   EXIT
6. GMA =   GMAC
7. KW   =   Keller Williams
8. PRU =   Prudential
9. RMX =   RE/MAX
10. IND =   Other local or national competitors
11. DIS =   Limited service or discount competitors

Table 9: Competitor Reconnaissance Worksheet

Part 2: Marketing to the Public: Company Services

Services	US	C21	CB	ERA	EXT	GMA	KW	PRU	RMX	IND	DIS
1. All listings advertised in local paper weekly											
2. All opens advertised weekly in local paper											
3. Company advertises on local radio											
4. Company advertised on cable television											
5. Company advertised on national television											
6. Company has national relocation services											
7. Company has international relocation services											
8. Company has offices in other countries											

Table 10: Competitor Reconnaissance Worksheet

Part 3: Marketing to the Public: Agent Services

Services	US	C21	CB	ERA	EXTA	GMA	KW	PRU	RMX	IND	DIS
1. 800 Call Capture System											
2. Weekly markeing evluation program using Call Capture statistics											
3. Customized marketing plan including targeted, nich marketing strategies											
4. Local cable television advertising											
5. Local radio advertising											
6. Ads in local home magazine											
7. Just listed cards (by mail)											
8. Traditional open house											
9. Broker open house											
10. 24-7 web open house											
11. Invite-a-friend open house											
12. Hand-delivered open house invitations											
13. Handwritten lead follow-up notes											
14. Showing Survey at the property											
15. Color brochures & brochure box											
16. 360 virtual tour CD/DVD brochure											

Table 11: Competitor Reconnaissance Worksheet

Part 4: Marketing on the Web: Company Services

Services	US	C21	CB	ERA	EXT	GMA	KW	PRU	RMX	IND	DIS
1. Listing appears on local company web site											
2. Listing appears on national company web site											
3. Company provides on-line buyer-seller matching service											
4. Company website accesses all local Multiple Listing Service listings											
5. Multiple Listing Service available in other languages											
6. Company website available in other languages to attract out-of-area buyers											
7. Company first page placement on major search engine (Google, Yahoo, or MSN)											
8. Company website has top local Alexa placement											
9. Company website gathers visitor email addresses											
10. 24-7 web open houses on company website											
12. 360 tour on company website											

Table 12: Competitor Reconnaissance Worksheet

Part 5: Marketing on the Web: Agent Services

Services	US	C21	CB	ERA	EXT	GMA	KW	PRMU	RMX	IND	DIS
1. Listing posted on Realtor.com											
2. Listing posted to personal website											
3. Separate website with the property address as the URL											
4. Agent's website accesses Multiple Listing Service											
5. Agent's website gathers visitor e-mail addresses											
6. 800 Call Capture number on agent website											
7. Autoresponders for immediate response to web inquiries on agent's website											
8. Pay-per-click advertising to reach buyers											
9. Agent belongs to a major buyer lead generation company											
10. Marketing program for buyers from lead generation company											
11. 24-7 web open house											
12. 360 tour on agent website											
13. 360 tour on CD brochure											
14. Listing posted to Global Estates website											
15. Drip e-mail marketing campaign											

Table 13: Competitor Reconnaissance Worksheet

Part 6: Customer Service

Services	US	C21	CB	ERA	EXT	GMA	KW	PRU	RMX	IND	DIS
1. Staging services											
2. Marketing Pledge assures customer satisfaction											
3. Transaction coordinator expertly assists in closing the transaction											
4. Corporate risk management program limits exposure to costly litigation											
5. Moving assistance services simplifies the moving process											

Table 14

The Strategic Marketing Plan

Virtually all sellers want to achieve the highest price possible for their property in the shortest time. Our unique Strategic Marketing Plan provides maximum exposure to the marketplace that will result in a higher price for you. Here's how it works.

1. Top List-to-Sell Price Ratio: Sellers who list with our company achieve a higher percentage of their list price as compared with other companies. This means even when they pay a full commission, our sellers actually net more than if they listed with another agency or sold "For-Sale-by-Owner."

2. Maximum media exposure includes radio, local cable television, and prominent advertising in local papers.

3. Our 800 Call Capture System guarantees we obtain an accurate telephone number from almost every person who calls on your sign, ad, or other piece of advertising. In contrast, other companies rely on agents to answer the phone. When this is the case, the agents answering the phone lose over 90 percent of the leads their advertising generates.

4. Top search engine placement and top ranking on Alexa.com. When buyers search for web listings, having first page placement on the major search engines means more buyers will see your property.

5. Most agent and brokerage websites have no way to harvest names from web visitors. Our free on-line classes, E-coupons, and on-line buyer and seller matching services assist us in obtaining good contact information from most people who visit our websites.

6. Global marketing strategy includes listing on six different websites plus providing our local Multiple Listing Services on-line in 12 different languages. This means we reach local, national, and international buyers for your property in their native language.

7. Unique open house marketing program includes hand-delivered open house invitations to neighbors and residents of nearby move-up areas. It also includes an "Invite a Friend" open house we host for your friends and family who may know potential purchasers for your property. Our 24-7 on-line open houses allow web visitors to view your home from the convenience of their own computer any time, any place.

8. Staging services help your home look its best. This in turn increases the potential price for which your property will sell.

9. Corporate Risk Management Program limits your exposure to costly litigation.

10. A virtual tour of your property plus digital photos will be posted on six different websites. These will also be available on CD for distribution during showings and open house.

Full Service Brokerage Means
More Dollars in Your Pocket!

You can use the Strategic Marketing plan in two different ways. First, you can include it in your pre-listing package. If you do this, use the plan in Table 14. If you use the Strategic Marketing Plan during your listing consultation, use the version in Table 15. Review each service with the sellers. Explain how these services help them obtain the highest price possible. After reviewing each item, ask the sellers what items they would like to include in their customized marketing plan. Asking the sellers what services they want is a way to do a presumptive close. Each "Yes" they give you takes you closer to listing the property.

(Please note: the Strategic Marketing Plan in Table 15 has more services than the one in Table 14. This is for illustration purposes. When you construct your plan, choose only the services you offer.)

During your listing consultation, you will use the Strategic Marketing Plan to explain what you and your company do to help the seller obtain the highest price possible for their property in the shortest time. Use the following script:

> *In order to obtain the highest price possible in the shortest time, you will need maximum exposure to the marketplace.*

(Hand them the Strategic Marketing Plan)

> *This Strategic Marketing Plan outlines how to achieve that goal. Which of these services would you like to use in marketing your property?*

After explaining each item, place a check mark by the services the seller selects. If the seller asks you to discount, the premium services such as 800 Call Capture, maximum media exposure, global marketing web program in multiple languages, the four types of open house, virtual tours, and posting the listing on six different websites would not be included. If you effectively demonstrate the value of these items, most sellers will pay a full commission to obtain these premium services.

Table 15
Sample Blank Strategic Marketing Plan
(Complete this during your listing consultation)

Services	Seller Wants
Top list-to-sell price ratio	
Maximum marketing & media exposure includes local cable TV, radio, & print advertising.	
"Never miss a lead" Call Capture technology	
Company has first page placement on major search engines (Google, Yahoo, & MSN)	
Top local company placement on Alexa.com	
Listing posted to Global Estates website	
Staging services	
Customized marketing plan	
Targeted/niche marketing program	
Color brochures delivered to other brokers	
360 tour	
360 tour on CD brochure	
Video e-mail marketing service	
24-7 web open house	
Invite-a-friend open house	
Hand-delivered open house invitations	
Call agents with listings in same area & move-up areas to promote listing	
Call agents with buyers who work this area to promote listing	
E-mail brochure to agents with buyers & listing agents who work this area	
E-mail brochure to agents with listings in move-up areas	
Handwritten lead follow-up notes	
New home competition strategy	
Moving assistance services	

Battle Plan #2
25 Reasons Our Company Sells Your
Property Faster for More Money

Battle Plan #2 differs from Battle Plan #1 in that you actually include your services alongside the services your competitors provide. As you construct your list, omit items your competitors offer that you do not provide. Better yet, take steps to offer these services. Once you identify the services you will use, construct your own checklist. The first column lists your services with an "X" adjacent to each service offered. The remaining columns should include the services your competitors provide. Place an "X" in each box for each service your competitors offer. While you can include all 50+ items on the Competitor Reconnaissance Guide, this strategy works best if it is limited to a single page. A sample is included in Table 16.

Table 16

25 Reasons Our Company Sells Your
Property Faster for More Money

Services	US	C21	CB	ERA	EXT	GMA	KW	PRU	RMX	IND	DIS
1. Top list-to-sell price ratio	x										
2. Complete media marketing program including radio, cable television, and print advertising	x										
3. Customized marketing plan including targeted niche marketing strategies	x										
4. Never miss a lead Call Capture technology	x										
5. Four types of open house including 24/7 web open houses.	x										
6. 360 virtual tour brochure on CD and website	x										
7. Listing posted to six different websites	x										
8. Company provides on-line buyer-seller matching service	x										
9. Company website accesses all local Multiple Listing Service listings	x										
10. Multiple Listing Service available in other languages on company website	x										
11. Company website available in other languages to attract out of area buyers	x										
12. Company has first page placement on major search engine (Google, Yahoo, or MSN) for local area	x										

Table 16 continued on next page

Table 16 Continued

Services	U S	C 2 1	C B	E R A	E X T	G M A	K W	P R U	R M X	I N D	D I S
13. Company website has top local Alexa placement	x										
14. Listing posted to Realtor.com	x										
15. Listing posted to personal website	x										
16. Agent's website accesses Multiple Listing Service with IDX or VOW	x										
17. Multiple Listing Service available in 12 different languages on agent's website	x										
18. Agent belongs to buyer lead generation company	x										
19. Pay-per-click web advertising to reach buyers	x										
20. Neighborhood website attracts local buyers	x										
21. Staging services	x										
22. Marketing Pledge assures customer satisfaction	x										
23. Transaction coordinator to expertly close the transaction	x										
24. Corporate risk management program limits exposure to costly litigation.	x										
25. Moving assistance services simplify the moving process	x										

You can use the Twenty-five Reasons handout in your pre-listing package. During your listing consultation, you can also review the five to seven key points that differentiate your services from those of your competitors. Use the following script:

In order to obtain the highest price possible in the shortest time, you will need maximum exposure to the marketplace.

(Hand them the Twenty-five Reasons)

This list outlines 25 different services that will help you achieve that goal. The five most important of these are (list your five key differentiating points). May I explain how each of these helps you achieve this important goal?

(Chapters 16 to 20 have additional scripts explaining key services referenced in the script above.)

If the seller asks you to discount, give the seller a modified checklist with only 10 or 15 services rather than 25. Make sure you include key services the competition offers plus one or two services they do not offer. Again, if you or your company has the top list-to-sell price ratio, most sellers will want your services because they will net more money.

You are well-armed and prepared to launch your attack. Now is the time to march into action.

Sellers Don't Save the Commission, They Earn It!

Jackie Leavenworth, Real Estate Coach & Trainer
Cleveland, Ohio

A very effective strategy for overcoming the discount commission objection is to offer the option of limited service. This is a "foot-in-the-door" strategy to get an appointment. The real benefit to us is that when a seller calls on the phone to ask us about commission, we can simply reply with:

> *That depends on your property and the services that you choose. I'll need to see your home and explain our service options. What time is convenient for you?*

People like choices. Sellers can opt for full service or they can save over half the commission by handling their own marketing. With the limited service option, we help them price their property, stage it, and assist them from negotiation to closing. We do everything except the marketing. Before making the decision, however, we coach sellers to educate themselves as to what is involved in the marketing process. The first step is to study the marketing services included in our full service option and to understand the importance of a varied market approach in order to attract the maximum pool of buyers.

"More buyers, more money" is my motto! Armed with that philosophy, we give sellers a list of questions that will help educate them as to their true costs and efforts.

> *Mr. and Mrs. Seller, earning part of the commission by marketing your own home is certainly one of your options. It is difficult to make an informed decision without the information. Therefore, it would be wise to do your homework and become aware of the*

process as well as the costs involved. Here are some questions to consider.

1. *Which local and regional newspapers and/or magazines will you choose and what is the weekly cost?*

2. *Who will write your ads and how will you know which media is effective?*

3. *What is the cost of television advertising to reach the largest market place?*

4. *On which websites will your property appear?*

5. *How many pictures can be uploaded?*
   a. *Can you have a virtual tour?*
   b. *What is the cost per week, month, quarter, etc.?*
   c. *How many unique users visit the site?*

6. *More than 80 percent of all homes sell through real estate professionals. What strategies will you use to reach the real estate brokerage community?*
   a. *If your home is in the MLS, what will you pay if a real estate professional finds your buyer?*

7. *How will you market, stage, and conduct your open house?*

8. *How available will you be to answer the calls, close the buyers for an appointment, and be present for the showings?*

9. *What process will you use to confirm that buyers are financially capable of purchasing your home?*

Getting the buyer to call is only the first step. Getting the buyers to show up and to commit is a learned skill. There are a few great books that may be of help that I am happy to recommend.

As a coach, I don't recommend supplying the answers. Let the sellers experience how much work it is just to finish this exercise, let alone to market their own home.

Most limited service brokerages charge an up-front, nonrefundable fee. When a seller is leaning toward this type of program, I find the following script works quite well.

I want you to imagine that you are about to file a lawsuit. You visit two different attorneys. Both tell you that your case is excellent and you should win. The first attorney charges $285.00 an hour. You pay the fee, win or lose. The second attorney will charge nothing for his time and expenses unless he wins or settles the case on terms acceptable to you. The question is which attorney would you choose to represent you?

The sellers always say they would take the attorney that doesn't charge. At that point, I draw the following analogy:

Our full service package is a turnkey option where my company and I assume the entire burden of cost and time to market your property. If we don't sell your home, we work for free. When you pay your marketing costs plus an up-front, non-refundable marketing fee to my company or to a competitor, you have a substantial investment in time and dollars spent. You will never recoup that money if your home does not sell. You have options. Please educate yourself and make the best business decision for you.

One of the agents in my program shared a fun experience. She made a great listing presentation and educated the seller with the questions above, but still lost the listing to a limited service company. Three months later, the seller called to list her property saying, "I should have listed with you in the first place, that was the biggest mistake I ever made."

The bottom line is that sellers almost always choose the full service option when they have a complete understanding of the time, effort and costs of handling the marketing themselves. Help them realize that commission dollars aren't really "saved." Instead, they are earned through the seller's attempt to do our job. It's really simple, they can hire me to do it for them, or they can pay themselves to do my job. And my job isn't easy!

Launch Your Attack

War does not determine who
is right—only who is left.
—Bertrand Russell

Chapter 16
The Waging War Listing Consultation
Part 1: Final Preparations

In war there is no substitute for victory.
—General Douglas MacArthur

Once you complete your competitor reconnaissance and decide on your unique, winning services, you are ready to weave it all together in the Waging War listing consultation.

Before you meet the seller, you must decide whether you will be using a one-step or two-step listing consultation. Ideally, it is best to preview the property, return to your office to prepare your consultation materials, and complete the comparable sales data. If you are able to do this, then a two-step listing consultation will work best for you. Many times, however, you may only have one opportunity to see the seller. In general, the best course of action is to prepare for a one-step consultation and conduct a two-step consultation when possible.

A second issue you must address if you are competing against another agent is to determine whether you will do your consultation first or last. The challenge with going first is the seller may want to speak with other agents before signing with you. If one of your competitors goes last and the seller wants to move forward, they may elect to sign with the agent because it's expedient. On the other hand, if you are the last agent, an agent before you may obtain the listing before you ever meet with the seller. If you plan to implement the strategies in this book, the smart move will be to go first. This puts you in the position of setting the bar for the competition. In most cases, they will have difficulty competing.

Listing Consultation Checklist—
Overview of What to Do Before the Appointment

Being prepared is more than having the right scripts and strategies. You must also prepare all the other supporting documents. The better your preparation is, the more likely you are to obtain a signed listing with a full commission. The checklist below is an excellent place to start.

____ 1. Check legal ownership. All legal owners must sign the purchase documents, even though your state may only require one signature for the listing to be valid.

____ 2. Check for bedroom-bath count as well as for improvements without proper permits. Know what your city or county requires when the improvements do not have proper permits as well as any potential penalties.

____ 3. Prepare a color brochure as the cover page for your listing consultation materials.

____ 4. Load the digital photos and other information about the property to a private area on your website so the seller can see what their property will look like on the web.

____ 5. Do your Competitive Market Analysis. Be sure to check "property history" to see if the property has been on the market recently and if so, at what price.

____ 6. Determine if you are in a sellers' market, buyers' market, or flat/transitional market by checking the inventory. If the market has less than six months of inventory, you are in a sellers' market where prices are probably increasing. If you have seven or eight months of inventory, you are in a flat or transitional market. More than nine months of inventory indicates a buyers' market where prices normally decrease.

____ 7. Customize and sign your marketing pledge. Remember to under-promise and over-deliver. (A sample Marketing Pledge can be found in Appendix A.)

____ 8. Prepare a sample 90-day marketing plan for the subject property.

____ 9. Identify at least five past sellers who are willing to recommend you. Include these testimonials in your listing consultation package. Be sure you obtain the past clients' permission to give out their names and phone numbers.

___10. If you are using search engine placement data as part of your consultation, print out hard copies to include during your consultation.

___11. Select your "Battle Plan" from one of the two Plans outlined in Chapter 15. The plans are summarized below:

a. "The Strategic Marketing Plan" (Table 15).

b. "Twenty-five Reasons Our Company Sells Your Property Faster for More Money" (Table 16).

___12. Documents to take on your listing appointment.

_____ a. Agency documents

_____ b. Listing agreement (also called Exclusive or Exclusive Right to Sell)

_____ c. Federal disclosure forms including lead-based paint

_____ d. State and local disclosure forms

_____ e. Local retrofit requirements (i.e., smoke detectors, low flow showers and toilets, etc.)

_____ f. If your company offers mortgage, title, or escrow services, you may be required to have your clients sign an additional disclo sure statement regarding these services.

_____ g. FIRPTA documentation. FIRPTA stands for Foreign Investment in Real Property Tax Act and requires the closing agent to withhold taxes for those individuals who do not have U.S. citizenship and/or Social Security numbers. Check your company's policies

> regarding the handling of clients who are foreign investors.

_____ h. Seller authorization for lock box or keysafe.

Once you complete your final preparations, you are ready to march forward.

Chapter 17
The Waging War Listing Consultation
Part 2: Take Aim

Don't just stand there.
Make something happen.
—Lee Iacocca

Listing Consultation Outline

You have identified your USP, have discovered what to expect from the competition, and have created an extensive plan to win the consumer. Now is the time to bring your forces together to win the battle. An overview of the entire consultation is below.

Part 1: Making the Connection

From the time you walk through the front door, you have only a few minutes before the sellers make a judgment about whether they would like to do business with you. Building rapport and creating connection are the two foundation pieces upon which your success or failure will hinge. You create rapport by being genuinely interested in the sellers and their property. More importantly, this is an excellent time to apply the 80-20 rule. Spend 20 percent of your time asking questions and 80 percent of your time listening to the sellers' responses.

____ 1. Begin by thanking the sellers for the opportunity to discuss the marketing of their home.

____ 2. Ask the sellers what they enjoy most about their property. Inquire about property features that may not be apparent to buyers during a walk-through of the premises. This can include upgrades such as insulation, hot water circulation system, or facts about the neighborhood.

____ 3. Take notes as the sellers tell you what is important to them about marketing their property. This sends a nonverbal message that you are genuinely interested in what they say.

____ 4. Ask the sellers about their plans for moving. If the sellers are staying in the area, ask if they would like you to represent them on the purchase of their next property. If the sellers are relocating, ask if they would like your help in finding an agent to represent them in their new area.

____ 5. Ask the sellers about any concerns they may have about listing their property. Once they have voiced their concerns, review your "Marketing Pledge" (Appendix A) that allows the seller to cancel the listing if you do not deliver the services you promised.

____ 6. Address Agency issues if your state requires this as part of the initial conversation. If your state does not specify when the agency discussion must occur, you can have the agency discussion as a prelude to signing the listing.

Part 2: Differentiating Your Services

____ 7. Review what all brokers do. ("Five P" Approach: Put a sign in the front yard, Place the property on the MLS, Put an ad in the paper, Place it on the web, and Pray it sells.)

____ 8. Explain that you want to assist the sellers in obtaining the highest price possible in the shortest time. To do this, you will use the Strategic Marketing Plan or the Twenty-five Reasons as outlined in Chapter 15.

____ 9. Review the plan you select during the next step of your listing consultation. This is where you will discuss, "What my company does that is different" and "What I do that is different." Show the sellers how your unique services help them obtain the highest amount of money for their property in the shortest time. During the review, make sure you discuss the three most impor-

tant services your company provides and the three most important services you provide to help the seller achieve this goal. As
you discuss these services, explain how each service helps the
seller obtain a higher price in less time.

____10. Presumptive Close: If you use the Strategic Marketing Plan from
Chapter 15, ask the sellers what services they would like to include in marketing their home. Place a checkmark next to each
service the sellers want. If the sellers ask you to discount later in
your consultation, you have three choices. You can provide the
seller with a reduced list of services for a reduced commission,
you can attempt to close them on the value of full service, or
you can walk away.

Call Save-a-Bug!

Ginny Hillenbrand, Burgdorff ERA, Realtors®
Parsippany, New Jersey

As Vice President and Director of Training for Burgdorff ERA, Realtors®, one of the key points I emphasize is the importance of discussing the unique services our company provides. These services are the basis for earning a full fee. Not only do our clients have a global presence through ERA, they also have access to one-stop shopping for title, mortgage, relocation, home warranty, and other ancillary services. In addition, we have two outstanding programs our competitors do not provide. The first, the Seller Security Plan, allows sellers to obtain money from their equity prior to the sale. They can use this money to purchase another property. Their buyers may also use the plan to purchase without contingency. When their home sells, they receive the balance of the money. If the home sells for less, there are no additional costs. If we can't sell it, ERA will buy it! The program understandably has parameters, but for the seller or buyer who fits the profile of the program, it's a real estate blessing!

The second program is our Select Lifestyle Services. This is the ultimate in concierge services. Other companies offer on-line access to contractors and other services clients may need when they move. Rather than relying on a website, our program assigns a specific point person who coordinates the annoying and time-consuming aspects of their move. All our clients have to do is call our toll-free number. Select Lifestyles Services will assist them in handling everything from staging their property, arranging for the movers, changing their address, turning the utilities on or off, or just about anything else they need. In fact, we even arranged for a Sunday haircut! That's what you do when a desperate, relocating client has an important interview on Monday.

The most outrageous example was a homeowner who woke up to find THOUSANDS of ladybugs in the wall. You wouldn't want to kill them! How much bad luck would that be moving into a new house? Our Select Lifestyle Services coordinator tracked down a "save-a-bug" service that transplanted the entire colony. Result? Happy Homeowner!

Amazingly, even with ALL these great support services, our agents are still sometimes asked to give a discount. I train them to handle the objection by looking the seller directly in the eye and saying,

> *No. I charge a full fee and I'm worth every penny of it.*

Recently, a new agent had an appointment with a For-Sale-by-Owner she had been courting during my class. He insisted on discounting her fee because he had other agents who would do it for less. She looked directly into his eyes and explained exactly what she knew about her value and the extraordinary services she could provide:

> *My fee is a percentage of the purchase price and though it sounds like more, I will not cost you more because of my expertise and ability to negotiate on your behalf.*

He signed the listing at full fee and it sold quickly at a price that astounded him. She received a letter praising the wonderful job she had done. Ultimately at closing, sellers get what they pay for and agents get what they believe they're worth!

Part 3: Market Statistics:
How to Realistically Price the Property

____11. Explain to the seller whether you are in a seller's market, flat market, or buyer's market. As a rule of thumb, markets with six or less months of inventory are sellers' markets. Seven to nine months of inventory indicate the market is flat or transitional. Over nine months of inventory indicate a buyers' market.

____12. Review the appropriate comparable sales to assist the sellers in determining their list price. Specifically, explain how appraisers set prices based upon closed sales, not list prices. Consequently, to sell their property at the highest price possible in the least amount of time, the sellers must list their property near where other closed properties have sold.

____13. Explain the "honeymoon period" (i.e., that most viewings of the property will occur during the first 30 days the property is listed) and then ask the sellers to set the price. Remind them that if they test the market with a higher price, they will probably miss the opportunity to capitalize on the high number of showings during the honeymoon period. If the seller still insists on a higher price, ask them to agree to a price reduction when the property has been shown ten times or listed for 30 days with no offers.

____14. Overcome the price objection by using the "Your house has to qualify" dialogue. (Instead of using the term "price," explain to the sellers their house must "qualify" with the lender. Lenders look at closed sales prices rather than listing prices to determine value.)

____15. If you have not done so already, explain agency and obtain the seller's signature.

____16. Ask the seller if they have any additional concerns or questions. Handle any objections.

___17. Fill out the listing agreement, including the full commission. (It's usually wise to have most of this completed prior to the time you meet with the seller.)

The smart agent will avoid the commission objection by outlining their services during the consultation. The following chapters explain critical components you must use to avoid the commission objection in the first place.

Chapter 18
The Waging War
Listing Consultation
Part 3: Fire Away!

He will win who, prepared himself,
waits to take the enemy unprepared.
—Sun Tzu Wu

You can have the best technology tools, the best systems, and the best customer service, but if you cannot articulate the benefits to the seller, then you have no real competitive advantage. Below you will find a series of scripts and strategies that can help you circumvent the commission objection entirely. Your success depends directly upon how effectively you master the scripts and how carefully you conduct your competitor reconnaissance. The section that follows focuses on the part of your consultation that discusses your USP.

Capitalize on Your Competitor's Weaknesses

Your first line of attack during your listing consultation utilizes your competitor reconnaissance to differentiate your company's services from those of the competition. While you can list services your competitors provide, it is normally more effective to concentrate only on three to five key differences. The primary theme during your consultation is:

My goal is to help you obtain the highest price possible in the least amount of time.

Because so many companies claim, "We're Number One!" sellers generally ignore such claims. Instead, what the sellers really want to know is "What's in it for me?" In other words, you must show the seller the benefits they will receive from working with your company rather than trying to persuade them how great your company is.

Begin your conversation by discussing "What all brokers do" using the following script:

Is it correct to assume that you would like to get the highest price possible for your property? (Wait for reply).

If the Seller answers, "Yes," you will continue your conversation. Before going on to the balance of those scripts, note that occasionally a seller may answer the question with a resounding, "No!" If the seller answers "No," then follow up by asking,

Did I understand that correctly? Achieving the highest possible price for your property is NOT a goal you want to achieve?

If the seller says they do not want the highest price possible for the property, it is extremely important to investigate the seller's underlying motivation. For example, some sellers may want to minimize their gain because they are retiring, going through a divorce, or the property is in probate. Others may be doing something much less honorable. If the situation makes you feel uncomfortable, pass on taking the listing. Becoming embroiled in a messy situation can negatively affect all aspects of your business. If your intuition tells you this seller is not a good fit for you, LISTEN to it! Our business is stressful enough without having to cope with nasty, miserable, or dishonest people.

Assuming the Sellers say they want the highest price possible for their property, continue the dialogue using the following script:

To obtain the highest price possible, you must have maximum exposure to the marketplace. All brokers will place your property in the MLS, put a sign in the front yard, and advertise on the web and in print media.

This script begins the discussion of your USP by outlining what all brokers do. The next step is to explain your personal USP. This will include a discussion of the unique services both you and your company provide.

At this point in your listing consultation, you will implement either Battle Plan #1 or Battle Plan #2. No matter which approach you select, be sure to identify the services the seller wants as well as explaining the key services that differentiate you from competitors. To keep your momentum during your consultation, remember to focus on approximately three to five key differences. In general, the more you talk, the more likely you are to encounter objections. Be concise, answer questions, and stay focused on what the seller wants and needs.

Reports from the Field
Show the Sellers How Important It Is to Get Their Property Closed

Nancy Sanborn and Lucy Matsumoto
Prudential California Realty, Beverly Hills, California

When we do a listing presentation, one of the first things we want to discover is the seller's motivation. Most sellers want to move quickly. Because interest rates are starting to increase, we explain how the interest rate increases influence the seller's price. With each interest rate increase, fewer buyers can qualify to purchase the property. A smaller pool of buyers translates into lower prices and longer market times. Worse yet, if the interest rates increase while the property is under contract and the buyers have not locked in their loan, they may not be able to qualify.

The same is true for the increase in prices. As prices climb, fewer and fewer people can qualify to purchase. Increasing prices and increasing rates can cost the seller money in several ways. If the seller is trading up, they may be unable to qualify for the home they could have purchased six months ago. Longer market times usually translate into lower sales prices and increased holding costs. If the market softens, sellers may find they have fewer buyers and that their property is worth less.

Consequently, it's important for the sellers to close as quickly as possible or lose potential buyers. One way we convert our seller leads into signed business is to show them our average market time. None of our listings has taken more than seven days to sell. This statistic alone is usually enough for sellers to sign the listing with us.

We also provide sellers with an extensive marketing plan, including how we market to the public and how we market to other agents. This helps our sellers achieve a higher price. When we look at the comparable sales for sellers who listed with a limited service broker, we find properties listed in the $300,000 to $400,000 price range generally received anywhere from $10,000 to $40,000 less than what the comparable sales data suggests. Not only did listing with the limited service broker cost the seller money in terms of market time, they received substantially less money as well.

Sellers need to know the market is constantly changing. If interest rates increase or if prices continue to rise, there will be fewer buyers for the seller's property. Once the seller decides to list, placing their property under contract as quickly as possible is usually the best course for everyone involved.

Don't Tell Them, Show Them!

Just to review, here are the scripts to use when you discuss the Strategic Marketing Plan and the Twenty-five Reasons.

For the Ten Point Guide with the Strategic Marketing Plan:

In order to obtain the highest price possible in the shortest time, you will need maximum exposure to the marketplace.

(Hand them the Strategic Marketing Plan)

This Strategic Marketing Plan outlines different services to help you achieve that goal. Which of these services would you like to use in marketing your property?

For the Twenty-five Reasons:

In order to obtain the highest price possible in the shortest time, you will need maximum exposure to the marketplace.

(Hand them the Twenty-five Reasons)

This list outlines 25 different services that will help you achieve that goal. The five most important of these are (list your five key differentiating points). May I explain how each of these helps you achieve this important goal?

Once you have explained the key points of differentiation, ask:

Which of these services would you like to use in marketing your property?

The discussion below provides ten examples of how to discuss key points of differentiation during your consultation. In general, you will lose the sellers' attention if you discuss more than three to five items. You may also appear pushy. Remember, your goal is to be concise and keep the consultation moving. You can use the scripts from the preceding chapters or use any of the scripts below. Mastering these scripts will help you to articulate your USP more clearly.

Sample Strategy #1: Top List-to-Sell Price Ratio

To use this strategy in your Waging War listing consultation, prepare your list-to-sell ratio as outlined in Chapter 13 and prepare a flyer like the one in Table 6. During your consultation, use the following script:

> *An important point to consider when selecting an agent is to determine their ability to obtain the best price for the properties they list. As you can see from this list-to-sell price ratio, our company has the best record of helping sellers obtain the maximum net proceeds for their property. Sometimes sellers believe saving money on commissions will net them more. As you can see from this chart, this is not the case in our marketplace. Instead, the best way to achieve the highest price possible for your property is to list it with a full service brokerage that provides maximum exposure to the marketplace. Is achieving the highest possible net dollar for your property a service you want?*

Virtually all sellers will answer, "Yes" to this question. At this point, you may be able to close the sellers without any additional conversation.

Sample Strategy #2: Strike a Decisive Blow with Call Capture

As discussed in Chapter 6, Call Capture is the most important technology tool you can use to convert a lead into a signed listing with a full commission. Follow the steps below:

1. Prior to your listing consultation, record a message on your Call Capture system giving a detailed description about the property. Be sure to include bedroom-bath count, attractive amenities, and anything else that would motivate a buyer to look at the property. Set up the system to forward your calls to your cell phone.

2. During the actual consultation, explain how over 90 percent of all sign calls and ad calls to most offices are lost because the floor broker is not adequately trained to obtain the lead's telephone number. Use the following script:

Another important factor to consider in selecting an agent is to determine how effective they are in obtaining accurate contact information from advertising. In order to obtain the highest price possible for your property, it's important to obtain a good phone number for every lead that calls on your yard sign, print advertising, and web advertising. Did you know that over 90 percent of these leads are lost because the agent answering the phone does not obtain the caller's phone number? Would you like to see how my system captures the correct phone number for virtually every person who calls on my 800 number?

Assuming they say, "Yes," then continue:

Please call the following 800 number and push the following extension.

While the sellers are doing this, turn on your cell phone. The sellers will generally be excited when they hear the message describing their property. About 30 seconds after the sellers hang up you will receive a phone call. Hand them your cell phone and ask them if the number looks familiar. This is usually enough to close them on the spot. In case the sellers have an unlisted number and are curious about how you generated their number, use the following script.

Because you called my 800 number and I paid for the call, I am entitled to access your telephone number. The great thing about this system is that it also generates accurate addresses for the caller about 60 percent of the time.

If your competitors do not provide Call Capture technology, ask the sellers to call on a competitor's listing and see how the agent handles the call. Since the person receiving the call typically fails to obtain a valid phone number, this strategy usually eliminates most competitors. Failure to convert telephone leads means less exposure for the property. Less exposure means less money in the sellers' pocket. In contrast, Call Capture technology allows you to follow up immediately when the buyer's interest is greatest. Thus, the seller can easily judge who is the most efficient at obtaining phone numbers and following up quickly. More importantly, rather than relying on what you or the other agent tells them, the seller learns firsthand who is the most efficient at capturing leads. If the seller is still skeptical, use the following script to close:

You have an important decision to make. You can list with an agent who lacks Call Capture and whose company may lose up to 90 percent of the leads their advertising generates or you can make sure your property has maximum exposure to the marketplace by using Call Capture. The choice is yours, what would you like to do—lose valuable leads or capture the phone number of virtually every person who calls on your ads and your sign?

Sample Strategy #3: Call Coordinator

If you do not have a Call Capture system, a slightly different alternative is a Call Coordinator. The Call Coordinator screens incoming ad and sign calls. These individuals are normally not licensed. Their primary function is to obtain the caller's phone number so a licensed agent can respond to the caller's questions. If your company provides this service, have the seller call on one of your listings to see how the system works. Then have the seller contact a competitor to see what happens in most offices. In most cases, the lead will be lost because the agent is unable to close for the phone number. In contrast, call coordinators usually obtain a correct phone number. By having the seller call your competitors and then call your office, the seller has a firsthand experience of how each company will handle buyer calls on their property. Here's the script:

Many companies advertise your property on the web and in the newspaper. Did you know that in most offices 90 percent of those leads are lost since the person answering the phone fails to obtain the caller's number?

(Wait for a response)

To obtain the highest price possible for your property, your real estate company must capture every potential lead. Our company has a call coordinator who obtains our callers' contact information. Before you list your property, call my office and those of any of my competitors to see who does the best job in obtaining your phone number. Is that a strategy that works for you?

If the seller says, "Yes," offer to step outside while they make the phone calls. If the seller says, "No," probe for the reason by asking,

Did I understand you correctly? Does this mean you are not concerned about losing leads for your property?

If the sellers say they are unconcerned, chances are they will not list with you.

Sample Strategy #4: Corporate Risk Management Program

Chapter 13 introduced the Risk Management Checklist. Sellers often have tunnel vision when it comes to reducing commission. They focus exclusively on the commission and ignore the other costs in the transaction. Few sellers consider how much a poorly trained agent can cost them at the negotiation table. While negotiation errors can be costly, disclosure errors or making inaccurate statements can jeopardize the seller's entire equity position. The beauty of the Risk Management Checklist is it explains potential disclosure pitfalls while simultaneously providing the seller with strategies to avoid these pitfalls. Best of all, it is a key way to establish yourself as the consummate professional who will protect the seller's most valuable asset.

To use this powerful tool in your consultation, take out the Risk Management Guide and hand it to the seller. Use the following script:

My company's Risk Management Guide can help you limit your exposure to litigation while also assisting you in achieving the maximum net amount for your property. Is limiting your exposure to litigation a service you want?

If the seller says, "Yes," continue with your consultation. If the seller says, "No," ask for clarity.

Did I understand correctly? Did you say you are not interested in avoiding costly litigation?

If the seller says, "Yes, we are not interested in avoiding legal difficulties," pack up your materials and leave.

Sample Strategy #5: Customized Marketing Program

The strongest defense you can mount against discounting is forming a strong connection with the seller. One way to achieve this goal is to allow the seller to select the postcards, ads, type of brochures, etc., they want to use to market their property.

Asking the seller for input strengthens your personal connection. In addition, having the seller select marketing materials is a critical part of a presumptive close. To utilize this approach, use this simple three-step strategy.

1. Choose three marketing strategies your competitors do not provide. Select three additional strategies your competitors provide that you will include in your marketing plan.

2. Create a list of these items including samples of different types of print advertising, postcards, e-mail marketing pieces, virtual tours on CD, etc. Have the seller select the materials they would like to use to market their property.

Use the following script:

A strong marketing plan is critical to achieving the highest price possible for your property.

Hand the seller(s) the Strategic Marketing Plan

As you can see from my Strategic Marketing Plan, there are a number of options in terms of postcards, e-mail cards, CD virtual tours, etc., from which to choose. Many sellers enjoy selecting the marketing materials we will use to market their property. Is creating your own customized marketing program a service you want?

If the seller says, "Yes," go through each item you have selected and see if the seller would like to include it in their program. Be sure to avoid over-promising. Again, when the seller starts picking out marketing materials, there is a high probability you have captured the listing.

Sample Strategy #6: Front Page Search Engine Placement

If you work for a major real estate company, your company's web page has a distinct advantage over those posted by local independents, especially in terms of buyers who live outside your immediate area. People who are relocating normally search the major brand name sites for listings outside their area. National companies generate national and international traffic. Consequently, they also rank higher on the search engines. What this means is national and international buyers are more likely to find your listings when you work for a national firm. If your company has excellent search engine placement, incorporate this into your listing consultation with the following script:

> *This printout from Google (and/or MSN, Yahoo) shows that our company consistently comes up on the first page of the search. When buyers find what they are looking for on the first page of their search, they seldom scroll down any further. Listing with our company provides page one exposure for your property. Is being listed with a company with first page search engine ranking a service you want?*

If the seller says, "Yes," you probably have the listing, especially if your competitors do not show up on the first page of your search.

Sample Strategy #7: Top Alexa.com Ranking

As discussed in Chapter 10, Alexa can be a powerful tool when working with sellers. To prepare for your listing consultation, print the pages with the Alexa graphics or, if you are using your laptop during the consultation, take the seller directly to the Alexa website to see the differences on-line. Because web rankings are so volatile, printing out the results will prevent surprises during your consultation. For example, your competitor may be running an event or promotion that drives above-average traffic to their site the day of your listing consultation.

To incorporate this into your listing consultation, determine the "rank" and "reach" statistics for both your company and any competitors. If you and your competitors both have Alexa traffic rankings in the top 100,000 websites, you can print out the traffic ranking charts and include the numbers in your discussion of web marketing. If neither you nor your competitors have top 100,000 ranking, use the traffic ranking by itself. Remember, the lower the number on the traffic ranking, the more visitors the website receives. To discuss Alexa traffic rankings, use the script below:

This web traffic analysis by Alexa.com shows that our company's website has more web traffic than any of our competitors. Is listing with a company that can give you maximum Internet exposure a service you want?

Another important Alexa statistic you may want to share is "Reach." Reach refers to the number of people who click through to your website for every one million hits using the Alexa toolbar. One reason to use reach rather than rank statistics is some sites may have agents or their FSBO clients visiting the site repeatedly to change their listings. You can modify the script above to discuss Reach, rather than Rank.

Did you know that over 73 percent of all buyers now use the web to search for property?

Wait for the response and then continue.

This analysis from Alexa.com shows that as compared to other companies in our area we have the most web visitors. Maximum exposure on the web helps you achieve maximum price. Is listing with a company that can give you maximum Internet exposure a service you want?

If you have a discounter causing you difficulty, be sure to print out their Alexa rankings as well. Assuming their Reach and/or Rank statistics are poorer than those of your company, use the following script:

Many discounters rely primarily on the web to market your property. In today's competitive market, obtaining the maximum price for your property means having both strong traditional and web marketing. Listing with our firm provides you with both. This translates into more exposure, less market time, and a higher price. Is having a strong traditional and a strong web marketing program a service you want?

Strategy #8: More Web Exposure Means More Buyer Exposure

Searching the web is like searching for a needle in a haystack. To increase the probability web visitors will see your listings, post them on as many high-traffic websites as possible. Two obvious places are Realtor.com and your company's website. The research from Realtor.com shows the most important thing to web visitors is plenty of pictures. If you post the seller's listing to multiple websites and provide numerous pictures plus a virtual tour, you will be ahead of most of your competitors. Use the following scripts:

An excellent way to achieve the highest price possible for your property is to make sure it is posted on as many websites as possible. Each property I list is posted on Realtor.com, the number one real estate website. In addition, your listing is also posted on my personal website, my company's local website, our national website, and our local Multiple Listing Service website. I will also set up a website with your property address as the web address. Is having your listing posted on six different websites a service you want?

You may want to also add:

Research from Realtor.com shows that web visitors skip over properties with only one picture and spend the most time looking at properties with multiple pictures and virtual tours. Visit www.Realtor.com and look at this property address.

(Include the link to one of your current listings.)

While you are there, you may want to investigate how other agents post their listings. The big difference, as you will see, is every one of my listings has at least ten pictures plus a virtual tour. Is having plenty of pictures plus a virtual tour something you want on all six websites?

Sample Strategy #9: Staging Services

Offering staging services is an excellent way to differentiate your services from those of your competitors. Depending on whether you provide the services yourself or use a decorator, pick the appropriate script.

To show your house to best advantage and to help you obtain the highest price possible, I provide complimentary staging services to all sellers who list with me. Is staging your house a service you want?

OR

To show your house to best advantage and to help you obtain the highest price possible, I work with a decorator who provides a complimentary consultation on how to make your house look its best. Is having a consultation with a decorator a service you want?

Sample Strategy #10: Open House 24 Hours per Day!

As discussed in Chapter 5, open houses can be a powerful tool for overcoming competitors. Again, be careful not to promise the seller more than you can deliver. Some sellers may expect you to hold their house open every Sunday. If you are carrying two or more listings, this is an impossible expectation to fulfill. The easiest way to circumvent this expectation is to use the 24-7 Open House strategy. Use the following script:

One of the most effective ways to market your property is with a 24-7 Open House. To make your property available to web visitors, I will post at least ten digital pictures plus a virtual tour of your property on my website. This allows buyers to see your house 24 hours a day, seven days a week, without ever having to disturb you. It's also an excellent way to reach buyers who are considering relocating to our area. Are 24-7 Open Houses a service you want?

You may also want to add:

Most sellers like to select the photos that will be posted to the website. Is being able to select the pictures to be posted on the website a service you want?

If the sellers say, "Yes," there is a high probability you have the listing. Again, if the sellers ask you to discount, ask them which items from the checklist they would like to delete in order to reduce the commission.

If you elect to do a traditional open house, prospect prior to the open house by hand-delivering invitations. Alternatively, use the "Invite-a-friend" open house discussed in Chapter 7. Here are the scripts:

In addition to the 24-7 open house, it's usually a good idea to hold at least two traditional open houses the first month the property is listed. Prior to each open house, I will hand-deliver invitations to your neighbors. Is having a traditional open house with hand-delivered invitations a service you want?

OR

An excellent way to market your property is through an "Invite-a-friend" open house. This open house is exclusively for your friends and acquaintances. If you will put together a guest list and select a date, I will handle the other details. The invitations will ask your guests to invite a friend who may be interested in purchasing your home. Is having an Invite-a-friend open house a service you want?

Again, if the seller says "Yes," there is a high probability that you have closed them on listing with you.

Check with your office manager to see what other services you can include. Remember, avoid going through a long list of services. Instead, choose three to five services the competition does NOT provide and focus only on those. Stay focused on what your company does that competitors do not do.

Be Prepared for an Ambush

As good as your services may be, many sellers still try to negotiate full service at a reduced price. If the seller asks you to discount at this point in the consultation, determine if you will offer fewer services for a reduced fee or will walk away from the listing. Use one of the two following scripts:

> *The unique services we provide that will help you obtain the highest price possible in the shortest time are available when you list for six percent. If you would like to list your property for less than six percent, here is the list of services we provide for a reduced commission.*

After giving them the handout, continue by saying

> *You have an important decision to make. Do you want the unique services that will help you obtain the highest price possible for your property or do you want to run the risk of obtaining a lower net price to you by using fewer services? It's your choice. What would you like to do?*

OR

> *Obtaining the highest possible price for your property requires maximum exposure to the marketplace. I only work with clients who want full service so they can obtain the highest price possible for their property. Is obtaining the highest price possible for your property a service you want?*

If the sellers say they still want to reduce the commission and you will not discount, say the following:

> *I wish you the best in selling your home for the maximum price in the shortest time. Thank you for the opportunity to discuss the marketing of your home.*

In many cases, the sellers will call you back. Most want full service. Nevertheless, many will test you to see if they can negotiate your services at a lower price.

My Commission is Three Percent
Michael Edlen, Coldwell Banker
Pacific Palisades, California

The lowering of commissions may be a slow-creeping disaster. I experienced the major downturn in the early 1990s. Commissions then were six percent. When the market declined, there was a huge consolidation of major companies. Many mid-sized and smaller companies simply disappeared. Even with six-percent commissions, many couldn't survive the market downturn. Today, the average commission is 5.5 percent or perhaps even less. The market has been excellent here for the last seven years. Unfortunately, the next major slowdown may have serious consequences for many firms, especially with 10 to 16 percent reduced commission rates.

I am a full service broker. When sellers ask me what my commission is, I generally respond by saying:

> *My commission is three percent. I recommend that you pay the cooperating broker who represents the buyer of your home three percent as well. When the other agent receives a full commission, the agent is more likely to do everything possible to keep the transaction together when the going gets tough.*

If the sellers focus only on one small part of the transaction (i.e., the commission), they may be opting to receive limited services. When this occurs, I ask them whether they are concerned more with the commission or with how much they will keep when the transaction closes. The sellers must decide whether they want to maximize their net profit or if they want to minimize their costs. Sometimes the sellers have a narrow focus. They only see the commission rather than looking at the entire transaction and the final bottom line. If the sellers focus only on the commission, I give them a choice. They can list with me for a commission we can both agree to. Alternatively, I often offer to give them the names of several other agents who will take the listing for much less. In fact, if they really want to save money, I suggest that they sell the property themselves. I will show them how to position their signs, where to advertise, and give them the name of a lender who can pre-qualify their buyers. At this point, most sellers back off and say they want a strong agent to represent them.

Regardless of the price point, I endeavor to charge a full commission because my team provides many more services than those provided by the average agent. I have invested heavily in staff support and advertising in order to create enormous benefit and exposure for my clients. When sellers list with me, they receive tremendous exposure in local and regional newspapers. I do a lot of direct mail. We also pay for two or three of the eight "Featured Homes" spots on Realtor.com for our area. Rather than running just a single exterior picture on the web, we post as many pictures as possible. We provide more color imagery in both traditional and web-based sources than do any of our competitors. Even for the higher priced homes, full service with extensive marketing exposure allows my clients to make the maximum amount from the sale of their home.

You have made a strong argument for earning a full commission. What do you do, however, when the seller says, John from your office offered us the same services for a five percent commission? How will you cope with this "traitor"?

Chapter 19
Trouncing Traitors within Your Ranks

It is unpleasant business to eject
a skunk, but someone has to do it.
—Chicago Tribune Editorial Board

Most sellers will want the services you provide. Nevertheless, many will try to negotiate with you to obtain the same services at a reduced commission. The next four chapters provide the additional ammunition you may need depending on who your rival is. To be fully prepared for all contingencies, it would be smart to master the dialogues below. You may need to overcome the discount objection several times before the seller finally agrees to give you the listing at a full price. As Margaret Thatcher put it, "You may have to fight a battle more than once to win it."

The discussion below provides additional ammunition when your Waging War listing consultation needs reinforcement.

CAVEAT: DO NOT OVER-PROMISE!

An old adage says, "Never use a cannon when a fly swatter will do." Putting it a little differently, there is no need to launch into all the information below unless the seller is being particularly resistant to signing a full-commission listing. When this is the case, listen carefully to their objections, and "fire" using the specific strategy that most effectively answers the objection.

Hanging "Benedict Arnold"

If you have ever done a bang-up listing consultation, one that emphasizes all the wonderful benefits the seller will receive from working with your company, and then, just when the sellers are ready to sign they say:

John Smith from your company was here earlier today. He offered exactly the same services you offer, except he said he would do it for five percent. We really like you. We will give you the listing provided you take a five percent commission.

The question is do you give in or are you strong enough to eliminate the most insidious of all discounters, the agent in your own office who is willing to cut their commission as a strategy to force you out of the competition?

There are several strategies you can incorporate into your battle plan to overcome this objection. Sometimes all you will need to defeat "Benedict" is a powerful script like any of those below.

Script #1:
In order to obtain the highest price possible for your property, you will need someone who is a powerful negotiator—isn't that correct?

(The obvious answer is, "Yes.")

So if you hire an agent who can't even negotiate a full commission on his own behalf, how effective do you think he will be in negotiating the maximum price for your property?

At this point, sit still, be quiet, and wait for the seller to respond. In most cases, the sellers will see your point and agree to a full six percent listing. The key point to remember when using this strategy is this:

"The first one who speaks, loses."

Be patient and wait for the sellers to respond to your close.

Script #2:
A slightly different script achieves the same results:

Hmmm, so John was willing to lower his commission by 17 percent. Is that correct? Would he be willing to give away 17 percent of your equity as easily as he gave away 17 percent of his commission?

Again, wait for the sellers to respond. Remember, "The first one who speaks, loses."

Script #3:

The next script emphasizes how the brokerage community reacts to listings that do not have a full commission. Before you use this script, you must be very careful to avoid price-fixing. The law REQUIRES you to emphasize that commissions are negotiable. Your role is to show the seller how listing at a full commission is a benefit to them. The script below works well when there is a great deal of inventory on the market. If you are experiencing a sellers' market, however, the other scripts and strategies are a better choice.

When the seller asks, "Why should we pay a full commission when other agents charge less?"

Respond by saying:

Because there is so much inventory on the market, you must price your house and your commission competitively in order to make it stand out.

Show them the percentage of listings that are at full commissions.

As you can see, the large majority of properties are listed at six or seven percent. If you were an agent and there is plenty of inventory, which listings would you show first?

Wait for their reply. In most cases, they will answer that they will show the houses with the higher commissions first.

Thus, you have an important decision to make. Will you list your property at a price and at a commission that will make it stand out or will you list it where it may not be competitive with the other properties on the market? The choice is yours. What would you like to do?

Script #4:

For those agents who have no attachment to obtaining the listing and who have no doubt about the benefits they provide, the following script can work to deflect the commission objection. The key in using this script is to avoid being flippant or sounding smug. Instead, say this in a quiet, even voice with no inflection. When the seller asks, "If commissions are negotiable, why won't you reduce yours?"

Respond by saying:

Yes, commissions are negotiable—would you prefer seven percent, eight percent, or perhaps ten percent?

Smile when you hand them the pen. Again, the key in using this response is to keep your voice neutral and your body language still. Any hint of sarcasm with the seller will probably cost you the listing.

Script #5:
Another time you are vulnerable to the discount objection is when you have a buyer for one of your own listings. This is also an issue if your company offers an "in-house incentive" (i.e., you earn a higher commission when you sell one of your company's own listings). When the seller says. "We will list at six percent. If you have your own buyer for the property, we want you to take five percent."

Respond by saying:

Unfortunately, I am unable to do that due to the Multiple Listing Service regulations. You see, if a buyer can get a reduced price from me and not from the competition, the Multiple Listing Service has deemed that to be an unfair advantage. This means I have to publish in your listing that I can sell your property for less money than other agents. The result is other agents will not show your property. Therefore, you have an important decision to make. Do you want to publish the "unfair advantage" in the MLS or do you want as many agents as possible to show your property? The choice is yours. What would you like to do?

Script #6:

You can use a slightly different version of the script above when you represent the seller on their listing as well as their next purchase. When the seller says, "If I list and buy from you, will you reduce your commission?"

Respond by saying:

By law, if you obtain a loan to purchase your next property and receive a commission rebate, you must disclose any rebate you receive to the lender, the other agent, and the seller. In most cases, when the sellers learn of the rebate, they want the reduction in commission to go back to them—not to you. The lenders do not like rebates because rebates often lower the buyer's down payment below the 20 percent level. Thus, you have a choice—add the commission rebate to the negotiation and have to worry about serious objections from both the seller and the lender or focus on getting the best possible price. It's your choice. What would you like to do?

Once the sellers respond, ask them to sign the listing agreement. If these scripts do not work, then it's time to roll out the heavy artillery.

The Big Lie vs. The Big Truth

Typically, the agent in your own office who discounts is willing to under-cut you by one percent. The first strategy you will use when another agent from your office attempts to capture the listing by discounting is to review the items listed below.

Each section below discusses the key issues from your perspective as an agent. (See Appendix A for information on how to obtain a customized Tips Booklet, *Who's the Best Person to Sell My House,* that incorporates the following information.)

The Big Truth

The "big truth" is that weak agents who discount often cost the seller money in a wide variety of ways.

1. *Agents who cut commissions usually have poor negotiation skills*

   An agent whose USP is primarily their discounted fee usually has poor negotiation skills. These poor negotiation skills translate into less money for the seller at the bargaining table. An effective negotiator can often negotiate an extra one percent on the seller's behalf, whether it is in the purchase price, inspections, or other terms of the agreement.

2. *Weak negotiation skills often result in overpriced listings*

   Agents who cannot negotiate full commissions typically have problems negotiating a realistic asking price. If the agent is unable to demonstrate the benefits of having a full commission, they will probably be unable to persuade the seller to price the property realistically. Consequently, agents who discount are more likely to take overpriced listings. This is a huge detriment to the seller, since most buyers will see the property during the first 30 days it is listed. After the first 30 days, activity drops dramatically and is limited primarily to new buyers coming into the market. Thus, if a property is overpriced during the first 30 days, the sellers will miss their best opportunity to obtain the highest price possible for the property. Not selling during this "honeymoon" period results in longer market time, price reductions, and in many cases, a smaller bottom line for the seller. By choosing a weak negotiator, the seller saves one percent. On the other hand, extended market time coupled with repeated price reductions can cost the seller as much as five to ten percent. On a $200,000 property, that is a net loss of four to nine percent or $8,000 to $18,000.

3. *Poor negotiators also cost sellers while the property is under contract*

   In addition to costing the seller money at the negotiation table, the seller faces further exposure based upon problems identified during the inspections. If the discounter cannot negotiate a full commission, then there is a high probability that they will also be unable to effectively counter buyer demands for additional repairs.

Repairs often cost thousands of dollars. Effective negotiation skills are critical to keep these costs at a minimum.

4. *Discount agents in your office usually offer poorer service*
Typically, it is the weaker agents who discount. In most cases, this means they also offer less service. For example, few discounters offer Call Capture technology. Since the typical floor broker fails to obtain a valid phone number over 90 percent of the time, 90 percent of the leads generated from sign and ad calls are lost unless your competitor has a call coordinator. Even when the listing agent receives the call, many are ineffective at converting the lead into a client. Thus, there is a high probability the buyer who would pay the seller the maximum amount for their property will purchase elsewhere simply because the discounter lacked the services and/or the ability to convert the lead into a signed offer.

5. *Less market exposure means a lower price*
In most cases, the agents who reduce their commission provide fewer marketing services than most full service brokers. This means the seller with a discounted commission receives less exposure, which in turn translates into a lower purchase price because fewer qualified buyers see the property. In many cases, less exposure costs the sellers much more than one percent.

6. *Less exposure also means longer market time and more carrying costs*
The less exposure a property has, the longer it usually takes the property to sell. Assume the seller saves one percent in commission, or $2,000 on a $200,000 property. If the sellers' carrying costs on the property are $1,500 per month, then taking an extra eight weeks to sell means that they will have $3,000 in carrying costs. Instead of saving $2,000, the seller actually ends up spending an extra $1,000 due to the additional carrying costs.

$2,000 savings
−$3,000 in carrying costs
($1,000)

(Carrying costs include market appreciation/depreciation plus principal, interest, taxes, and insurance.)

7. *Builder incentives create double trouble*

Higher commissions definitely motivate agents to show listings. In areas where builders actively compete with resale properties, builders often sweeten the deal with upgrades, interest rate buy-downs, and other perks. Many builders also happily pay agents a full commission. In this environment, discounting is deadly since not only is the new property a better deal for the agent, it is an even better deal for the buyer.

8. *Litigation and other post-close problems*

Lawsuits are a nightmare. They pull us off focus, cost us time and money, and make us miserable. Strong negotiators can usually avoid litigation because they can negotiate an acceptable solution to most disputes. In contrast, an agent's inability to reach a mutually agreeable solution to a dispute can tie the property up for years in litigation. Also, depending upon where the agent is doing business, attorney fees can be $50,000 just to prepare to go to court. Trials can cost considerably more.

Win the War, Not Just the Battle

Mastering these concepts will provide powerful protection from discounter attacks. In fact, if you clearly delineate how your services differ from those of your competitors and demonstrate the value of those services to the seller, this question seldom arises. Granted, some sellers may know you offer more than the other agent and still ask you to discount. If this is the case, return to your Strategic Marketing Plan or your Twenty-five Ways handout and ask the seller which services they want to eliminate in exchange for lowering the commission.

The next question is how to handle companies that discount.

Chapter 20
Overcoming the Big Lie:
Limited Service Brokerage Programs

Here's the rule for bargains. "Do other men, for
they would do you." That's the true business precept.
—Charles Dickens

"Limited Service Brokerage" programs provide sellers with MLS access, forms, signs, and in some cases, actual marketing materials. The seller shows their own property and normally negotiates their own deal as well. The seller may opt to pay a full commission to the buyer's agent or may elect to work only with principals. The typical savings are two to four percent. Using a $200,000 purchase price, the savings would be $4,000 to $8,000. This model can cost the seller in at least 12 different ways.

Sellers Just Think It's Cheaper— They're Wrong

1. Dangerous Showings
Having sellers show their own listings to unqualified buyers endangers not only the seller's pocket book, but their safety as well. Sellers are often unaware of the pitfalls of working directly with buyers. For example, smart agents never represent the exact location of boundary lines. Instead, the agent would advise the buyer to obtain a survey. In contrast, the seller may point out where they believe the boundary is located. If the seller makes an error, the seller can be liable for the buyer's reliance on that representation. Specifically, if the buyer built new improvements and had to remove the improvements due to an easement or encroachment, the seller would probably be liable for the survey costs, any legal costs, and substantial damages related to removing the improvements. In fact, the misrepresentation could result in a rescission of the sale.

Because they are afraid the buyer will not purchase, many sellers avoid pointing out problems. When the buyer asks about the condition of the property, the seller may say, "Everything is working normally." If problems occur during the inspections or after closing, the seller can be liable for the repairs because they represented "Everything is working normally." A seller who has to replace a roof, an air conditioning system, or make some other type of major repair can easily spend $5,000 to $10,000.

The worst risk, however, is not financial. A man was recently convicted in Austin for posing as a buyer and murdering a woman who was selling her home For-Sale-by-Owner. Because it is easy for most men to overpower a woman, female sellers are particularly vulnerable. Criminals often case listed properties as potential burglary targets. Unchaperoned open house visitors may dig through bathroom drawers and cabinets looking for drugs and other valuables.

In contrast, most agents insist that the sellers are out of the property during showings. This limits their exposure to litigation while simultaneously protecting the seller's family and their belongings.

2. Overpricing

The primary reason sellers use a Limited Service Brokerage is to save commission. Because the brokerage has minimal involvement, the seller has little motivation to price the property realistically. Since sellers normally lack access to closed sales data, they frequently base their price on what other sellers are asking for their properties. This results in overpricing. When the buyer asks the seller to justify the asking price, most sellers are unable to do so. Overpricing means longer market time. This results in lower purchase price, higher marketing costs, and increased holding costs.

3. Buyers Expect Discounted Fees to Benefit Them, Not Just the Seller

Bargain hunting buyers specifically target FSBOs as well as properties listed in Limited Service Brokerage programs for two reasons. First, bargain hunters expect to pay wholesale, rather than retail price. They know the seller is not paying a full commission and their goal is to capture those savings for themselves. Second, shrewd buyers know that most sellers are poor negotiators who will give price concessions not only at the negotiation table, but during the contract period as well.

4. Inability to Identify Qualified Leads

Inexperienced or poorly trained agents often fail to qualify the buyers by determining their wants and needs. Some agents take buyers out before determining whether they are qualified to purchase. This situation is even more prevalent when the seller works with the buyer directly.

Failing to qualify the buyer can have serious consequences. Almost everyone feels uncomfortable prying into someone else's finances. Many sellers are reluctant to ask whether the buyer has been pre-qualified by a lender. Furthermore, they are even less likely to ask for a letter from the lender indicating the buyer's price range. Second, sellers are often so eager to show their property, they fail to ask what is important to the buyer. Without this information, the seller can kill the sale by pointing out features the buyer hates. In either case, the seller wastes hours of valuable time showing their property to unqualified prospects. Worst yet, not knowing how to pre-qualify the buyer can result in the seller tying up their property with a buyer who cannot qualify for a loan. This translates into extended market time, additional carrying costs, as well as escrow, title, and other fees. In most cases, the defaulting buyer has no legal obligation to reimburse the seller for these costs.

5. Inability to Convert Leads into Showings

When someone calls on the seller's property, sellers often lose the lead since they have no experience using the telephone to motivate the buyer to look at their property. Instead, they try to persuade the buyer to see their property since it is the only thing they have to sell. By failing to ask about the buyer's needs, the seller often loses the lead. Sellers also lose leads by failing to ask for the caller's telephone number. In many cases, the prospect will want to "get back" to the seller. If the prospect does not call the seller back, their potential buyer is lost. There is no commission savings when there is no sale.

6. Poor Lead Follow-up

After each showing, listing agents routinely follow up with buyers and their representatives. In contrast, when the seller calls the buyer to follow up on a showing, the buyer may conclude the seller is desperate. This situation is even worse when the seller calls the buyer about a price reduction. For shrewd buyers, the seller's apparent desperation is an excuse to submit a low offer in order to explore how low the seller will really go. Rather than obtaining the highest price possible for their property, the seller may be looking at offers 5 to 20 percent less than they might have obtained under normal circumstances. On a $200,000 property, that translates into $10,000 to $40,000.

7. Lack of Experience in Overcoming Objections

In most cases, buyers will not discuss their likes and dislikes with the seller. Consequently, the seller really has no way to overcome the buyer's objections since the buyer never voices them in the first place. Even when the buyer does voice an objection, few sellers recognize that objections are actually buying signs. Instead, when the buyer objects to something about their property, the seller may become defensive or try to explain away the problem. In either case, the seller will rarely ask an effective closing question. Without being able to recognize buying signs and overcome the buyer's objections, the seller is not likely to make the sale. When the sellers cannot close the sale, they increase their holding costs while also increasing the probability that they will have to reduce their price.

8. Enforceable Contract

Most states have done everything within their power to minimize the amount of contract language an agent has to write. When an agent uses a form approved by their state, MLS, or local association, issues such as liquidated damages, arbitration, inspection, and a host of other potential problems have been addressed. While some Limited Service Brokerages provide forms for their sellers to fill out when they obtain a buyer, without adequate training the sellers can create a huge legal problem for themselves by failing to address contract issues properly. Thus, to protect themselves, sellers should have all documents reviewed by an attorney. The review can cost anywhere from several hundred to several thousand dollars depending on whether or not the attorney has to redraft the contract or extricate the seller from an incorrectly drafted agreement.

9. Liquidated Damages

When sellers negotiate their own transaction, they seldom use a liquidated damages provision. State law often sets liquidated damages (i.e., the amount the seller can keep if the buyer defaults for no reason). In addition, some states require the contract's liquidated damages provision to be set in a certain sized type. Failure to meet these requirements invalidates the provision. Even when the parties agree to a liquidated damages provision, there is still the challenge of handling the situation when the buyer defaults. For example, in California, even when both parties execute the liquidated damages provision, the buyer still has to sign an escrow amendment to release the funds to the seller. This can be sticky for experienced agents, and even more so for sellers. A trip to the attorney to resolve the dispute can easily eat up the three percent the seller would have received. Making matters worse, if the buyer is unwilling to cancel the transaction and fails to perform, the litigation to extricate the seller can cost thousands of dollars.

10. Inability to Handle Contingent Sales

In many cases, buyers purchasing a home will have to sell their existing property in order to close on the new property. If the seller accepts an offer contingent upon the buyer selling their existing property, the sellers have no control over when their property will close. This means they cannot accurately predict when they can close on a new property. If the transaction falls apart, the seller may be subject to payments on two properties or liable for defaulting on their new purchase. Furthermore, it will be difficult for them to recoup the costs they incurred while their property was under contract.

11. Lack of Experience Solving Transaction Problems

Even qualified buyers can have loan or title problems. In general, about 95 percent of all transactions have problems that threaten the closing. Of these transactions, 90 percent ultimately close, but only because an agent assisted the principals in working through the challenges. Because the sellers lack experience in solving transaction problems, their transactions often fall apart. Thus, instead of closing, the seller must start the entire process over again.

12. Agents Resist Potential Dual Agency Problems

When sellers do their own negotiations and handle their own transactions, the buyer's agent may have a mess with respect to agency. To close the transaction, the buyer's agent may have to handle issues normally handled by a listing agent. The challenge in this scenario is the buyer's agent is the exclusive representative of the buyer. If the buyer's agent advises the seller on what to do or how to do it, the agent may inadvertently create a dual agency situation. The agent may have breached their fiduciary duty to their buyer while also violating state agency regulations. The potential for being sued increases dramatically when the seller handles part of the transaction normally handled by the agent. To avoid this assortment of problems, many agents avoid showing listings where dual agency may be a problem. Unless the agent informs the buyer about their showing policies, not showing such a property can create its own set of problems.

While these 12 points can help you win consumers from Limited Service Brokers, the best strategy may be a simple script.

Reports from the Field
Discounters Are Wonderful!
Jerry Rossi, RossiSpeaks.com
Raleigh, North Carolina

Several years ago, I went on a listing appointment for an estate property in our area. The owners were a patent attorney and a pediatrician. The patent attorney was very stern. She wore a severe business suit, her hair was in a bun, and she had a dour look on her face. Selling her home was serious business. In contrast, her husband was very cordial and enjoyed laughing. He was the one who served us milk and cookies.

I did my normal upbeat, high energy listing presentation. It was happy, with plenty of free-flowing ideas on how to market their home. In the middle of the marketing discussion, the attorney interrupted in mid-sentence by saying,

We have a company that will do it for 2 ½ percent.

My response to her was,

That's great! Discount brokers play a very valuable part in today's real estate business for those who cannot afford premium service.

I continued with the presentation and obtained the commission at a full six percent.

Last week, one of my coaching clients invited me to go on a listing presentation with him. During the course of the presentation, the seller mentioned two discount agencies in their area. The agent responded with a slightly different version of the script I used with the attorney. When the seller asked about the discount brokers, he responded by saying:

Discounters are wonderful! They fulfill an important need in the marketplace for sellers who cannot afford premium service.

He listed the property at a full six percent. After the presentation, he thanked me for sharing that script with him. The agent said he had used this approach over one hundred times and every time the sellers listed at a full commission.

These are not the only enemies you will need to overcome, however. In many cases, your competition can be a local or national on-line real estate company.

Chapter 21
Overcoming the Big Lie:
On-line Discount Brokerage

The art of war is simple enough. Find out where
your enemy is. Get at him as soon as you can.
Strike him as hard as you can, and keep moving.
— Ulysses S. Grant

A corollary to the Big Lie is that placing property on the Internet will sell it. This is similar to saying that placing a property in the newspaper will sell it. Whether the seller places their property on the web or uses print advertising, these are simply vehicles for exposing the property to the marketplace.

Over the last few years, a new breed of discounter has emerged. These companies provide access to all MLS information using IDX or VOW provided the visitor registers on their website. In some cases, the on-line brokerage actually makes the MLS data appear as if they are displaying their own listings. The bitter battle over who owns MLS information and who should have access may not be resolved for years to come. From an agent's perspective, the real issue is how to earn a full commission when confronting an on-line discounter.

Eight Ways to Overcome On-line Competitors

To defend against on-line discount companies, capitalize upon the weaknesses in their model with the eight strategies below.

1. Connect to the MLS with IDX or VOW

To compete against on-line companies, you must link your website to your local MLS using IDX or VOW. To conquer on-line competitors, you must provide the same services plus much more. When a seller asks you about what makes your services different, use the Strategic Marketing Plan or the Twenty-five Reasons handout. Ask the seller:

> *Other than listing your property on the Multiple Listing Service, which of the following services does the on-line broker provide?*

If you have done your competitor reconnaissance, you already know the answer and have included services the other company does not have.

2. Personal Connection Trumps an Anonymous Website

Having access to the MLS is important in finding a property. It is no substitute, however, for personal connection. A website cannot tell the seller what to do when the buyer decides to ask for a new roof when a small repair will alleviate the problem. Websites are unable to calm first-time buyer jitters and certainly cannot solve that bizarre problem no one has ever encountered before. To overcome this objection, ask the seller the following question:

> *What strategy does the on-line broker have for solving transaction problems such as repairs, title problems, and mortgage problems?*

Let the sellers sit with this question, because the website cannot provide an answer. This means they have to speak to an agent and the issue then shifts to which agent can provide the best service.

3. Buyers Seek Exclusive Representation

Most buyers want someone who represents their interests exclusively. When on-line companies display MLS data so the listings appear to be their listings, they may actually lose buyers since most customers want exclusive representation. Thus, the website visitor may be *more* likely to search elsewhere for exclusive buyer representation. While some buyers certainly work with on-line agencies, many use the on-line brokerage to search for listings and then return to work with an agent with whom they have a personal connection. For most people, the purchase of a home is the largest financial transaction they will make. Asking a seller or buyer to trust someone they have never met before requires a big leap of faith. To point this out to the sellers, ask the following:

> *If you were buying a property, would you allow an agent you have never met before to be the person who represents you on the largest financial transaction you will probably ever make?*

4. Most Web Marketing is Passive

Web marketing using IDX or VOW is essentially passive rather than proactive. The company or agent who relies on people contacting them from a website has the same problem as the agent who relies on floor calls: they don't control their lead generation and they certainly don't control their income. Furthermore, just as most agents lack a specific strategy for converting floor calls into solid leads, most agents who harvest names from websites also lack a strategy to follow up consistently on those leads. In fact, web prospects may require up to 37 contacts before they will agree to do business with you! This passive approach coupled with poor lead follow-up puts these agents in the same category as a poorly trained floor broker.

5. On-line Still Requires a Human Who has Problem-solving Skills

Virtually no one purchases a property sight unseen. Thus, there must be face-to-face interaction when the buyer views the property. Someone must submit the offer and conduct the negotiation. Once the property is under contract, it still takes a human being to resolve transaction problems that occur in over 95 percent of all transactions. Sadly, most buyers and sellers believe the agent's primary job is to place properties under contract. Any experienced agent knows that 80 to 90 percent of the work occurs in closing the transaction, especially in resolving appraisal problems, title problems, credit reports, inspections, etc. One of the amazing things about the real estate business is no two transactions seem to "go wrong" exactly the same way. This is where the agent's problem-solving skills are critical. Agents who routinely close a high number of transactions each year develop excellent problem solving-skills. In contrast, many on-line brokerages are primarily order-takers. This means the agent taking the order is probably not as well versed in critical problem solving as an experienced traditional agent. Less ability to solve problems translates into longer market time and less money for the seller.

6. On-line May Limit the Seller's Exposure to the Marketplace

For some on-line brokers, exposure of the seller's property may be limited to exactly that—on-line on their company's website. If this is the case, the question is how well does the on-line broker drive traffic to their website as compared to a full service competing brand? If the on-line brokerage is receiving less traffic than the full service brokerage, then the seller is making a poor choice in terms of on-line marketing. If the on-line brokerage is not on the first page of Google or the other search engines, the probability someone will find their on-line listing is very low.

7. More Bang for the Buck

Another important question to answer is whether the on-line broker belongs to the MLS. Again, if the agent's role is to assist the seller in obtaining the highest amount possible for their property, the listing will need maximum exposure to the marketplace. Without MLS placement, the property will not reach the majority of the brokerage community. Clearly, this reduces the seller's ability to achieve the highest possible price in the shortest time.

8. Buyers' Agents Shy Away From Transaction Problems

Even when the on-line broker belongs to the MLS and offers a full commission to the selling agent, agents may be reluctant to show properties where they know they will have to do part of the seller's work. Sellers who have little if any experience in closing a transaction usually rely on the buyer's agent to cope with transaction problems. As noted above, agency is an additional problem. Depending upon state law, when the buyer's agent advises the seller on how to solve a transaction issue, the agent may have created a dual agency situation and conceivably violated their fiduciary duty to the buyer. Furthermore, sellers who are unfamiliar with disclosure laws and other mandated requirements are much more likely to create legal problems for all involved. When the seller fails to disclose or misrepresents something to the buyer and the buyer decides to sue, generally the broker is named, even if the broker did nothing wrong.

While listing agents are keenly aware of how they are being forced into commission compression on the seller's side, buyers' agents are now facing many of the same issues.

(See Appendix A for information on how to obtain a customized Tips Booklet, *Who's the Best Person to Sell My House,* that incorporates the information above.)

Waging War on the Buyer's Side

It is impossible to win the race unless you venture to run, impossible to win the victory unless you dare to battle.
—Richard M. DeVos

Chapter 22
Battling Commission Compression
on the Buyer's Side

The world does not pay for what a person knows, but
it pays for what a person does with what he knows.
—Laurence Lee

Thus far, we have concentrated on defending your commission on the seller's side. Agents who represent traditional buyers as well as those who work as an "exclusive buyer's agent" also have serious reasons to be concerned about how they handle discounting.

Buyers' Agents Beware!

If you work as a full service agent and you simply avoid showing properties with discounted commissions, you could be in for serious legal difficulties. As an independent contractor, you have the right to determine how you will conduct your business. Nevertheless, the phrase, "Commissions are negotiable" has implications for all agents. Specifically, if a group of agents agrees to avoid showing discounted listings, they can leave themselves open to charges of price-fixing.

Brokers who refuse to pay discount firms the same commission as full service firms may also be subject to the charge of price-fixing. This creates a difficult dilemma for the buyer's agent. The buyer's agent wants to act in the best interest of their buyer. This means acting in good faith to acquire the property for the buyer. If the buyer's agent challenges the listing agent's fee agreement prior to closing, the listing agent may persuade the sellers to work with a different buyer. If the fee dispute goes to arbitration after closing, the buyer's agent runs the risk of alienating the other agent and brokerage. This in turn reduces future cooperation that can translate into fewer sales.

When the buyer and the buyer's agent execute a Buyer's Listing Agreement, there can be additional problems. Under a Buyer's Listing Agreement, the agent has a fiduciary duty to the buyer. This includes finding the best property available for the buyer at the best possible price and terms. If the buyer's agent elects not to show "by owner" properties or properties with discounted commissions, then the buyer's agent may be violating their fiduciary duty to the buyer. Whether the agent works as a cooperating broker under an Exclusive Right to Sell or under a Buyer's Listing Agreement, the best way to avoid this issue is to disclose your showing policies in writing to the buyer. If the buyer agrees, then there is no issue. If the buyer has an issue, it is better to address it up front and resolve it before doing any work on the buyer's behalf.

Reports from the Field
If It's Not Listed in the MLS, You're on Your Own

Nancy Sanborn and Lucy Matsumoto
Prudential California Realty
Beverly Hills, California

We're currently in a very strong sellers' market where properties sell with multiple offers the first day they are listed. In many cases, the sellers receive more than asking price. As a result, we are experiencing more discounting of commissions. We are also seeing more activity from limited service brokers. The biggest problem with these agents is their lack of professionalism. Most of the time they don't return our phone calls, even when we tell them we have highly motivated clients.

Because we do a high volume of business, we often receive offers from these agents as well. Whether we represent the seller or the buyer, our experience has been we usually end up doing all the work. Because our area is so litigious, this is the only way we can protect our clients.

Our biggest challenge with limited service brokers is determining the exact commission. Our MLS requires the listing agent to state the commission rate to the selling broker. This policy circumvents most commission disputes. Often times, however, we discover new listings in the paper or at Sunday open house that are not listed on the MLS. This can be a very difficult situation.

For example, we had buyers who lost in multiple offers on three different properties. We located a property in the paper and spoke with the limited service agent. The agent informed us that the commission to the selling side was two percent. We arranged to show the property and wrote up the offer with a two percent commission to our firm. When we were ready to present the offer, the agent informed us that her "listing" was actually a For-Sale-by-Owner. She told us, "The sellers were paying two percent to me for bringing you in." Because this was the right property for our buyers, we rewrote the offer with a one percent fee to each company.

After this experience, we made a business decision only to show buyers properties listed on the Multiple Listing Service where the commission is in writing. We're so busy, it's better for us to pass on problem situations. When we begin working with a buyer, we tell them up front what our showing policy is—"If it's not listed the MLS, you're on your own." Sometimes our buyers purchase properties from an open house or an ad in the paper. If that happens, so be it. We want what's best for our clients and support their decisions. Besides, the hassles involved simply aren't worth our time.

Protect Yourself Against Landmines

As "Buyer's Agency" becomes more common, so will the need to defend your commission when you represent the buyer exclusively or when you sign a Buyer's Listing Agreement. At first glance, there seems little reason to be concerned. In reality, however, the dangers are like landmines—you cannot see them, yet when you step on one, it blows you and your transaction to smithereens. To understand the dangers, the first step is to be aware of the most common types of commission agreements as well as the potential dangers within each type. An agent who works as the buyer's exclusive representative has five primary options with respect to the commission. Each of these options has potential pitfalls.

1. *Agent works exclusively with buyers and collects the commission the listing agent posts on the MLS.*
   Pitfalls: When the agent works exclusively with buyers and collects the cooperating commission posted in the MLS, there is normally no difficulty. Agent compensation is identical to the arrangement under an Exclusive Right to Sell agreement. Occasionally, however, when an agent takes a discounted fee on the listing, they may attempt to split a four percent fee 50-50 even though they posted the buyer's fee as three percent in the MLS.

2. *The agent agrees to represent the buyer for a flat fee. If there is an overage, the buyer receives the difference.*
   Pitfalls: Flat fees create a host of difficulties when there is an overage that the buyer receives as a credit. The agent must disclose any commission rebate to all parties, including the seller and the lender. The question is, "When must the agent disclose the rebate to the seller and lender?" In virtually every case, the disclosure should be included in the purchase agreement. When the seller learns that there is a buyer rebate, most sellers are unhappy about paying it. If the rebate appears in the purchase agreement, most sellers will attempt to negotiate the price so they can recoup part of the rebate. More importantly, if the buyer uses the rebate as part of their down payment, it often lowers the buyer's down payment below the 20 percent level. When the buyer puts less

than 20 percent down, the lender may add Private Mortgage Insurance (PMI). This has the effect of raising the buyer's monthly payment until they do have 20 percent equity in the property. If the seller and the lender discover the rebate after the transaction closes, both parties can charge fraud. The lender may also have the option of "calling the loan" which means the entire loan amount becomes immediately due and payable.

3. *The buyer selects from a "menu of services" and the agent bases the fees upon the items selected.*
   Pitfalls: This situation is subject to the same Pitfalls as in "2" above. The buyer may elect to have more or fewer services. If this is the case, it is difficult to know the exact amount of the rebate until the transaction closes.

4. *The agent uses a rebate agreement to refund part of the commission to the buyer. This is especially common for discount warehouses as well as some lenders who rebate the buyer a portion of the commission.*
   Pitfalls: This situation can be particularly sticky since you now have a corporation directing the agent on how to handle the rebate. Check with your local board or with your state department of real estate to determine what is legal in your area. Certain states prohibit this type of agreement. Before entering into a referral agreement with a company that provides buyer rebates, be sure to examine their policies regarding disclosure carefully and to determine whether their policies conform to state and federal laws.

5. *The buyer and the agent enter into a Buyer's Listing Agreement.*
   In this case, the buyer pays the agent a commission in the same way a seller would under a normal listing agreement. The buyer and the buyer's agent have a fiduciary relationship. The buyer compensates the agent regardless of what the seller does. The buyer who agrees to an exclusive Buyer's Listing Agreement, generally has an advantage over the buyer whose agent represents the buyer under an Exclusive Right to Sell agreement. There are two primary differences:

a. Depending upon how the Exclusive Right to Sell agreement sets up the agency relationships, the buyers' agent may be obligated to help the seller achieve the highest price and the best terms possible. In contrast, in a Buyer's Listing Agreement, the buyer's agent seeks to obtain the best possible price and terms for the buyer.

b. When there is an offer, many buyers' agents allow the listing agent to present their offer to the seller. On the other hand, when there is a Buyer's Listing Agreement, the buyer's agent normally will insist on presenting the offer on behalf of the buyer rather than relying on the listing agent.

Pitfalls: Buyer's Listing Agreements create their own set of problems. Assume the seller agrees to pay the listing agent six percent under an Exclusive Right to Sell agreement and the buyer agrees to pay their agent a three percent commission based upon the purchase price. Theoretically, there could be a nine percent commission, since the listing agent earns six percent when the property sells. The question for the buyer's agent is how to handle the potential nine percent commission. Since the buyer's agent is not a party to the listing agreement, they have no legal right to ask the listing agent to reduce their commission. On the other hand, both the buyer and the seller would probably seek a commission reduction if they knew the total commission was nine percent. Agents working under a Buyer's Listing Agreement should check with their local Board of Realtors® as well as their management to determine how to handle this problem. At a minimum, the buyer's agent should ask the listing agent how the seller would like to handle the situation. Whether or not the listing agent discusses the situation with the seller, the buyer's agent should clearly state in their offer that the buyer is paying the buyer's agent's commission. In other words, there will be no "cooperating broker commission" on this transaction. Again, this is a very difficult situation since the seller has a binding contract with the listing agent regarding the commission amount.

More Minefields for Buyers' Agents

While Buyer Listing Agreements are growing in popularity, much of our industry continues to fight the practice. The primary fight occurs over "procuring cause." Procuring cause refers to the agent who introduces the buyer to the property and is the basis for determining who deserves the commission. Some areas use the "threshold rule" to determine procuring cause. This means the agent who first shows the buyer the property (i.e., the agent who is at the property when the buyer crosses the threshold) is entitled to the commission. If a buyer executes a Buyer's Listing Agreement with a different agent, the buyer's agent could do all the work and the original agent who showed the property would still earn the commission. Buyers' agents can protect themselves by having a clause that says the buyer will reimburse the buyer's agent for the commission should there be a dispute and a different agent is awarded the commission.

Buyers' agents can also protect themselves by refusing to negotiate on properties the buyers have seen with a different agent. This protects them against a wide variety of very sticky situations. For example, assume a buyer has signed a Buyer's Listing Agreement and the buyer walks into the open house hosted by the listing agent. If the threshold rule is in play, the listing agent is due the commission. This is a major disadvantage for the buyer since the listing agent has a fiduciary duty to achieve the highest price possible with the best possible terms for the seller. Even though most states allow buyers to designate their representative, this does not necessarily mean the buyer's agent will earn the full commission. The net effect is the buyer's agent has an increased risk of losing an agreed upon commission.

Nightmares from the Field of Battle

Because of the strong seller's market in most places in the country, some agents have taken desperate actions in terms of how they attempt to obtain listings. In other areas, changes in the law have now given both buyers and sellers free rein to ask for part of the agent's commission.

Pay Me a Referral Fee

For years, California law prohibited agents from paying non-licensed individuals a referral fee or commission rebate. Like many other states, California changed the law so commission rebates are now legal. The way you handle this situation depends upon whether the seller pays your commission through an Exclusive Right to Sell or through a Buyer Listing Agreement.

If your state prohibits paying non-licensed individuals any portion of the commission, tell your buyers that this is a state regulation. Never agree to do anything under the table. You are putting both you and your buyer at serious risk.

If your state allows commission rebates, be sure to disclose the rebate in writing to the seller. If the purchase is all cash, then this is the only required disclosure. When most sellers become aware the buyer is receiving part of the commission, however, they normally take steps to prevent this from happening.

If the buyer is obtaining a loan, the commission rebate must follow Federal guidelines set forth in the Real Estate Settlement Procedures Act (RESPA). RESPA requires you to disclose any commission rebate in writing to the seller, the other agent, and the lender. Failure to do so can result in criminal charges for defrauding the lender. Many buyers put 20 percent of the purchase price down when they purchase. A commission rebate technically reduces the buyer's down payment to less than 20 percent. Remember, this change may prevent the lender from selling the loan on the secondary market. This can cause the lender to call the loan "all due and payable."

When the buyer says, "Pay me a referral fee," be completely honest with all parties about the nature of your agreement and disclose it in writing.

"Commissions Are Negotiable"

What happens if you have a property listed at six percent and the buyer's agent writes a four percent commission into the offer? The buyer who actually did this argued, "Commissions are negotiable." Fortunately for the agents involved, the seller set the buyer straight regarding this issue. No matter whom you represent, "commissions are negotiable" up to the time you execute the Exclusive Right to Sell or a Buyer Listing Agreement. Once the parties execute the contract, it is binding on the parties and the commission is no longer negotiable. In this case, the buyer was attempting to induce the sellers to breach the contract they had entered into with the listing agent.

$1.00 Commissions and $1.00 List Prices

This is not a typo. A company in California actually lists property for $1.00 with a $1.00 commission. Obviously, this scenario seeks to create a bidding war on the purchase price. If the buyer's agent has a client who wants to bid on the property, the agent is stuck with the $1.00 commission. The solution to the problem is to collect the commission from the buyer. If the buyer has not executed a Buyer's Listing Agreement prior to this situation occurring, however, it is highly unlikely the buyer's agent will collect a commission. If the buyer does execute a Buyer's Listing Agreement, the buyer who works with an agent is still at a competitive disadvantage since the buyer will be paying more than someone who does not work with an agent. Agents who avoid showing these properties could arguably be engaging in price fixing. Buyers may also dump them "for not showing us everything in our price range."

I Won't Accept Your Offer

Recently an agent who specializes in probate properties bumped into a different version of the buyer agency problem. Her buyers wanted a specific property for which the sellers refused to pay a commission to a buyer's agent. She negotiated a Buyer's Listing Agreement. The listing agent and the sellers refused to accept any offer where the buyer's agent received a commission. Since the buyers still wanted the property, the agent honored what was best for the buyers and bowed out of the negotiation. Whether this situation violates any laws is unclear. There is a high probability that the listing agent and seller interfered with an established agency relationship. The agent could pursue an action, but since she handles a large volume of business, she decided it was not worth the hassle.

Separate and Not Equal

Discounters are bumping into a backlash nationally. Some full service brokerages now offer different cooperating broker commissions. For example, if a discount competitor shows a six percent listing, the discounter might only receive one percent. The listing agent may retain the other five percent. The same situation also occurs for many agents who are working under a Buyer's Listing Agreement. If the total commission is $10,000 and the buyer's agent has agreed to accept a commission of $2,000, the listing agent will retain the remaining $8,000. In cases where the listing agent negotiates a seven percent commission and the standard cooperating commission is three percent, some listing agents retain the full four percent.

While the situations above occur sporadically, it is more common for listing agents to reduce their commission and pay the buyer's agent a full commission while they "eat" the discount. For example, an agent takes a listing at four percent. To sell the property quickly, the agent lists the cooperating brokerage fee at three percent. This practice is especially common in a strong seller's market where there is little inventory and properties sell quickly, often with multiple offers. At the root of this problem is the misconception that the agent earns their money primarily for marketing the property. As discussed throughout this book, this misconception can cost the sellers considerably more than the amount they save by cutting the commission. Until more agents can articulate the benefits of full service, sadly these practices will remain in place.

A Winning Strategy for Buyers' Agents
Ideally, if each agent negotiated their own commission with their own client, we could circumvent many of the problems about the buyer's representation of the seller under a cooperating broker agreement as well as issues related to Buyer's Listing Agreements. If the seller wants discount service and the buyer wants full service, both parties would come out ahead. Consumers would have a higher level of protection since they would be able to choose the fees and the level of service they want. The fee arrangement would also increase confidentiality for both buyers and sellers. Whatever they negotiate is between the consumer and their representative. Nevertheless, as long as we continue to work under cooperating broker agreements, buyers' agents will be subject to whatever commission the listing agents select.

Chapter 23
Defending Your Turf

Nothing in life is as exhilarating
as to be shot at without result.
—Sir Winston Churchill

Even when we have negotiated a full commission, the moment there is a problem our commission immediately comes under attack. After all, if the sellers and buyers have to throw more money into the transaction to resolve a sticky problem, why shouldn't the brokers have to do the same thing? The strategies below can help you avoid being hit for additional commission or if you are hit, limit how much it hurts.

It's Their Property, Not Yours

Many agents create potential commission problems for themselves simply by how they discuss their listings and sales. For example, listing agents often make the following types of remarks:

I think your property should be listed at $249,000.

I think putting a sign in the front yard is a good idea.

When we sell your home…

When we receive an offer…

I think we should accept this offer.

I think we should ask the buyers for an earlier closing date.

The examples above all use "I" and""we" language. In each case, the agent's choice of words inserts the agent into the decision making process. The result is an open invitation to blame the agent when something goes wrong. When "we" make a decision and there are unanticipated costs, "we" are expected to share the costs out of "our" commission.

To avoid this problem, you must do two things. First, always use questions. When you ask what the seller would like to do, the seller feels in control. Clearly, people respond better when they feel they are in control rather than being told what to do. Second, instead of using "I" and/or "we" language, use "you" language and ask questions. For example:

The comparable sales for your property are between $245,000 and $255,000. Where would you like to position your property in the marketplace?

Having a sign in the front yard increases your exposure to the marketplace and can help you to achieve a higher price for your property. Is having a sign in your front yard a service you want?

When you sell your home...

When you receive an offer...

Is this an offer you would like to accept?

Would you like to ask the buyers for an earlier closing date?

Finally, the most important phrase to master is the following:

The choice is yours. What would you like to do?

This phrase gives the power back to the client and puts them in control. It will also help you avoid having to reduce your commission when things go wrong.

Damage Control

Once you have your buyers or sellers under contract, an important way to defend your commission is to have a conversation explaining what happens in most transactions. Specifically, 95 percent of all transactions have problems so severe that the principals believe the transaction will not close. Even so, 90 percent of these transactions *do* close. At this point, emphasize that you really earn your commission by keeping the transaction on track and trouble shooting any problems en route to closing.

One creative agent handled this situation by giving her buyers or sellers a box of beautiful chocolates when they placed a property under contract. Together they would open the box and enjoy a single piece. She then asked them to keep the rest of the chocolates. When problems occurred, she would call her clients and say, "It's time to have a piece of chocolate." The chocolate symbolized how "sweet" it would be when the problem was resolved and the transaction closed. This light-hearted approach was quite powerful for several reasons. First, when things go wrong, most people go into reaction mode by becoming angry or unreasonable. Eating a piece of chocolate gives all parties time to gain control over their reactions. Second, the chocolate serves as a "pattern interrupt." If the client is feeling angry, eating the chocolate interrupts the emotional pattern. Third, chocolate increases beta-endorphins. This in turn increases happiness and well being. Thus, the client is more likely to feel the issue can be resolved.

Regardless of how you introduce the problem, it is extremely important to put the client in control of the decision-making. For example, assume the driveway from the neighboring property is encroaching on your listing by six inches. Before speaking with your seller about the issue, check with your manager and the title company to explore all options. Find out how much it will cost to have the property surveyed to set a new property line. Examine what the sellers' options are for negotiating with the neighbors with respect to the encroachment. Once you have identified all the potential options, go to the seller and explain their choices. At the end of your explanation, ask the sellers:

Of these three options, which one works best for you?

This is a crucial point: it is their property and it is their decision. If they ask you for your advice, outline the potential solutions again. If they press you for your suggestions, remind them, "It's your property and it's your decision." The moment you advise them which solution to accept, you expose yourself to losing your commission if your solution fails.

Protective Armor

Sometimes sellers will ask you to reduce your commission during the offer negotiation process. A primary way to limit your exposure is to contact your manager. Since the listing agreement is between the seller and the brokerage, the only way to modify the listing agreement is with the consent of the supervising broker. If you cannot cope with the request to reduce your commission, referring the question to your manager can often circumvent the reduction.

If you are stuck reducing your commission due to a problem where both the buyer and seller are putting in additional funds, you can limit your exposure by asking to share the costs one-third for each party (i.e., the sellers, the buyers, and the brokers each pay one third.) A common trap many agents fall into is sharing the costs one-quarter each to the buyer and seller and one-quarter to each broker. This means the brokers are stuck with fifty percent of the cost, even though they are not party to the transaction.

To limit your exposure when things do go wrong, use the ten tips outlined below.

Ten Strategies to Defuse Difficult or Angry Situations

No matter how good your connection is with your seller or buyer, there are times when your principals or other people in the transaction may become very angry. When this happens, here are ten strategies to get through this difficult time.

1. When your clients become angry, take immediate steps to defuse the situation by first letting go of any need you may have to be right or to win.

2. When a client is yelling, do a "pattern interrupt." This technique comes from Neurolinguistic Programming (NLP). The strategy is to stop the angry behavior as quickly as possible. A pattern interrupt may be asking a seller who is upset about a low offer to get a glass of water for you. When the seller changes their body position, it can also change their mood. If someone is yelling, an excellent way to create a pattern interrupt is to ask them to pause

for a moment while you obtain a pen and paper to write down what they are saying.

3. In order to limit your risk, take careful notes on what is being said by anyone who is angry. After doing the pattern interrupt, ask the angry individual to repeat what they just said so you can write it down. Having the individual review what they have already covered usually reduces some of the anger. Take careful notes on what they say.

4. Next, ask the individual to pause. Read back what they stated in "charge neutral." Charge neutral means repeating what they said in a flat, unemotional tone of voice. Using charge neutral defuses the situation by removing the emotion from what the client says. This has a calming effect. Using charge neutral also reduces the client's anger level more quickly.

5. Ask the individual if you wrote down their concerns correctly. Then ask if there is anything else. Stay with the anger until the person has said everything they needed to say. Continue to repeat back what they say in charge neutral.

6. If the anger is directed at you, respond with:

   It was never my intention to make you angry. What can I do to correct the problem?

   Notice there is no acceptance or blame, only an effort on the part of the agent to take steps to correct something that has gone wrong.

7. If the individual is still extremely angry with you, offer to arrange a meeting with your broker/owner/manager.

8. If the anger is directed at someone else, avoid criticizing the other party. Instead, say:

   That's terrible. How can I be of assistance in solving this problem?

9. If you made a mistake, don't give excuses or say, "I'm sorry." "I'm sorry" requires an explanation. Instead say,

   Forgive me—I made a mistake. What can I do to rectify the situation?

   This puts the power in the hands of the other individual without excuses or rationalizations. It also shows your willingness to take responsibility for your actions.

10. When your client is unjustifiably angry, avoid arguing or trying to prove your point. If you cannot honestly say, "I understand your point of view," at least write down their concerns. Read back what you have written to make sure you captured your client's concerns correctly. In most cases, the client will calm down when someone takes the time to listen to them.

Whether you represent sellers or buyers, there is one more weapon you can use against competitors. This secret weapon may be the most powerful of all.

Chapter 24
The Ultimate Secret Weapon—
The "A-bomb"

Our deeds determine us, as much as we determine our deeds.
                                                    —George Eliot

So far, we have identified a variety of ways to overcome the discount objection. While each of these tools work, they are even more effective when coupled with the most powerful weapon of all. The secret weapon that can enhance every other strategy you use and is virtually unknown to most of your competitors is the "Principle of Attraction."

When I began my formal training as a coach in 1996, my initial response to hearing about "Attraction" was, "Yeah, right—there's no way that's going to work." Since then, I have heard hundreds of successful agents share how attraction helped them to dramatically increase their business while also significantly improving the quality of their lives.

Attraction is the foundation upon which long-term, sustainable business is built. In fact, most agents who have 15, 20, or 30 years of consistent top production use attraction rather than relying on scripts and techniques. These highly successful individuals understand the importance of professionalism, excellent service, and building strong relationships with their clients. In fact, when I speak to groups about the principles of attraction, the top producers usually are the ones who are most likely to "get it." They already use this approach naturally. On the other hand, those agents who are struggling often respond by saying:

> *Yeah, that's great, but how can I get more listings? What scripts do I need to use?*

Agents who rely solely on scripts and techniques will always have challenges because they are focusing on the tools rather than the connection with the client.

If you are unfamiliar with these concepts, what you are about to read may seem like a bizarre way to earn a full commission. In fact, some people actually become angry when asked to take an honest look at their lives through the filter of attraction. While the steps below may seem unrelated to earning a full commission, let me assure you, the "best of the best" use these principles to attract their top-notch clientele. To make yourself more attractive to higher quality clients who are happy to pay for your top-notch services, start working on implementing these changes in your life today.

The Five Core Principles of Attraction

Attraction can be broken into five key areas. For attraction to work, you must address each area. If after reading this, you are still skeptical, I challenge you to an experiment: use these principles for one month and see if your business improves. Chances are you will be surprised at the results.

1. *"We attract who we are"*

   If our personal lives are in chaos, we will attract clients whose lives are in chaos. If we are stressed out, we will attract clients who are also stressed out. While it may be painful, take a realistic look at whom you have attracted in your business. Are your clients completely loyal or do they end up dumping you for some inexplicable reason? Do your transactions go smoothly or are you always having one disastrous transaction after another? Do you attract truthful clients or people who misrepresent the truth? The concept of attraction explains why this occurs.

   a. First, the people we attract mirror what is occurring elsewhere in our lives. If you attract disloyal people, where have you failed to keep your word or do what you promised to do? If your transactions are always a minefield, where are you lacking integrity in the other areas of your life? To break this pattern, remember to always tell the truth and always walk your talk.

   b. The next step is to start taking better care of you. Be honest: how long has it been since you have taken off a full weekend? How many times have you had dinner with those you love in the past month? I used to work 12 to 14 hours per day until my coach nagged me long enough that I started taking time off to do some fun things for me. The result: my productivity increased by 50 percent. By taking time off to unwind, I actually accomplished more. The biggest surprise, however, was how all those "difficult" people in my life "magically" disappeared. Remember, a frazzled, stressed-out agent is not who most sellers or buyers want negotiating on their behalf. In contrast, caring for yourself makes you more attractive to both potential sellers and buyers.

Even when you are functioning at high levels of attraction, you can still attract dishonest or chaotic people into your life. The key is being able to recognize when someone does not fit your style of doing business. For example, how many times have you had that little voice inside tell you "don't take this listing" or "don't work with this buyer" and by not listening, you ended up with a disaster on your hands? Being able to say "No" is an important key to increasing your attraction and your production. Consequently, when that little voice inside says, "No"—listen to it!

2. *Create space*

Experienced agents know the moment they plan a vacation, business immediately picks up. In scientific terms, nature abhors a vacuum. When you create space in your business, more business usually shows up. On the other hand, if your schedule is already packed 24/7, your production will remain capped at current levels because there is no room for new business to come into your life.

This next suggestion may seem a little odd. I have given this assignment to thousands of agents and virtually everyone who does it sees an increase in their business. To make more room for new business, clean your closet, clean your desk, clean your garage, file those stacks of papers, fire those buyers who are wasting your time, and refer that listing you have had for 12 months to another agent. It makes no difference where you start. The goal is to eliminate whatever is easiest that is taking up unnecessary space.

The next point is extremely important. Creating the space for more business does not mean to stop working. Instead, it means getting rid of sellers who won't sell, buyers who won't buy, and people who waste your time and give you nothing back. It also means learning how to utilize the best technological tools currently available. Technology can dramatically cut down on the time, effort, and costs involved in operating a successful real estate business. Better yet, it gives you a huge competitive edge against those agents who lag behind in this area.

3. *Have clarity about what you want to attract*
What does it mean to have clarity about what you want to attract? An agent who had created a phenomenal income in just six months had this reply when I asked him how he did it:

The first thing I did was sit down and write a list of characteristics of my ideal client. It was 15 pages long, right down to the type of belt and tie he wore.

When I asked if his ideal client had shown up yet, his response was:

No, but a lot of his brothers and sisters sure have.

If you do not have a detailed list describing your ideal client, now is a great time to begin one. The more specific you are, the easier it will be to say "Yes" when the right sellers and buyers show up and "No" to those who are a poor fit because they are difficult, unreasonable, or dishonest. Surprisingly, the moment you say, "No," you actually increase your level of attraction. In fact, saying "No" to over-priced listings, to unethical sellers, or to sellers who are unwilling to pay a full commission actually increases the quality of clients you will attract. Again, the principle of attraction says, "like attracts like." In other words, when we have high standards and high ethics, we attract people who are like us. When we lower our personal standards because we are desperate for money or for business, we attract people who attempt to manipulate us and take advantage of us.

4. *Give back*

There's an old adage that says, "When you give to a giver what do they do? They give back!" If you constantly take from others without giving back, you will find that your business will require four to five times as much effort to make it grow. Agents who do not honor the principle of giving back constantly have to prospect for new business since they seldom receive referrals from past clients. The research shows that generating a new lead from cold prospecting takes five times more effort than generating a new lead from a past client. Take a hard look at your business. Do you give back in some way shape and form to both past and present clients? Are you contributing to your community? Remember, if you want people to "contribute" to your business, you need to "contribute" to others.

5. *The attitude is gratitude*

This final component of attraction can be summed up in a simple question:

How can I ask for more when I don't appreciate what I already have?

How many times have you expressed your gratitude to buyers or sellers for doing business with you before the transaction is closed? Have you ever told your office manager you appreciate the fact that he or she is there to help you? What about the people at the escrow or title company?

Unfortunately, many people in our business focus on what they lack rather than all the things they do have. For example, many agents believe top producers receive more than their fair share of leads from management. Whether or not this is true, when agents focus on the unfair distribution of referrals, they are not taking responsibility for actively building their own business. When they complain, they reduce their attractiveness to potential clients. This results in less income. This pattern can result in a dangerous downward spiral that can cause the agent to leave the business. In contrast, showing gratitude for what you have is an excellent way to be more attractive.

To avoid having this happen to you, take time to tell others how much you appreciate them. Along the same lines, take a few moments each day to record five things in your life that are really great—whether it's something as simple as your health, a roof over your head, clean water, or food. You can keep track in a journal, in your appointment book, or in your contact manager. A great way to start your day is to do this before you begin work. Remember, if you want more business or more of anything in your life, you need to appreciate and be grateful for what you already have.

When you encounter someone who asks you to "discount," in most cases the person is feeling "lack." Whether it is another agent or a seller, realize this person probably lacks abundance. Their response to you may be to try to bring you to their level (like attracts like) or they may envy what you have and decide not to do business with you. In other cases, they will be attracted to you because they sense you will attract a higher quality buyer for their property because of who you are.

We cannot change what other people feel about themselves, but we can increase our personal attractiveness. Attraction is your "secret weapon" against discounting. The "best of the best" want to do business with the "best of the best." Do everything you can to increase your personal attraction and rest assured, what shows up in your life will truly be amazing.

Reports from the Field
Are You One of a Thousand Guppies?
Lee Konowe, Marketing Director
Northern Virginia Fine Homes
Reston, Virginia

Earning a full commission is often a function of self-perception. When you have a discount mentality, you will attract people who want to discount. On the other hand, when you know your value, you are clear about the excellence you provide. Clients who want excellence are willing to pay what it costs.

I used to be a doctor. I never remember a patient on the operating table asking me if I could cut them for a little bit less. In fact, a great example of this point comes from the doctors doing Lasik surgery. Several years ago, doctors doing this procedure were engaged in a discount war. Instead of $1,200 per eye, the fees dropped to as low as $295 per eye. The hope was to make up the difference in volume. What the doctors experienced was the more they lowered costs, the more money they lost. Not only were they making less on each procedure, they were obtaining poorer outcomes. The patients they were attracting were more likely to complain and often required more post-operative care.

The same is true for the real estate industry. When you reduce your commission, you devalue yourself and the services you provide. This becomes a self-fulfilling prophecy. When you cut commissions, you often attract difficult people who are extremely demanding. You have poorer outcomes that require more work for substantially less pay. The more you cut, the more difficult it becomes to have positive outcomes.

In contrast, the higher your standards are, the more quality clients you will attract. For example, 20 percent of the transactions in our area fall apart because the financing did not happen. We never accept a contract until we verify with the lender that a buyer actually has the ability to close. Sellers are attracted to us because they know that once their house is under contract, the transaction will close.

Each agent has a reputation. Clients will be attracted based upon that reputation. You have the power to decide about what reputation you want. Will you be a beautifully colored guppy who stands out from the rest? Or will you disappear into the crowd of a thousand other guppies hoping you can make up your lost fees by being like everyone else?

Chapter 25
Crouch in Cowardice or March Nobly Into Battle

Cowards falter, but danger is often
overcome by those who nobly dare.
—Queen Mother, Elizabeth

You are about to make a decision that will affect your career from this point forward. Will you march nobly into battle? Are you willing to do what is required to capture the consumer's business and loyalty? Will you falter and give up the fight? The question you must confront is what action are you willing to take?

Waging War is your strategic battle plan for winning the discount war. Are you willing to do the competitor reconnaissance and make the fundamental changes necessary to reverse the commission compression trend in your career? Are you willing to make the shift from win-lose to win-win? If so, you will see an increase in your own production. You will be doing what it takes to win the war.

Alternatively, will you read the book, remark on the great ideas, and then put the book away and do nothing? Rather than surrendering, I challenge you to raise your own level of professionalism and service. Look back through this book and identify *one* change you will make today to do a better job the next time you are asked to discount. Now make that change!

If you currently have listings, implement an 800 Call Capture system to ensure you never lose a lead. Incorporate the Strategic Marketing Plan or the Twenty-five Reasons into your listing consultation and hit the competition with your "A-bomb." Remember, all it takes is three or four small changes to win the consumer. You can do it if you dare to take action.

When you choose to raise the bar in terms of your professionalism, consumer service, and excellence, you help to raise the bar for our entire industry. The more agents who commit to providing buyers and sellers with tremendous value, the harder it will be for those who lack these standards to compete. I encourage you to join me on this march toward excellence.

On a final note, I am extremely grateful to each of our readers. If you enjoyed this book, share it with a friend. Brainstorm ideas on what you can do to be more effective. If you have a great strategy you would like to share, please e-mail us at WagingWar@RealEstateCoach.com. Thank you again for being one of our valued customers. Now go out and "Wage War on Real Estate's Discounters!"

Appendices

Appendix A: Resources

*There will come a time when big opportunities will be presented to you,
and you've got to be in a position to take advantage of them.*

—Sam Walton

Appendix A is divided into four sections. The first section is devoted to supporting materials for this book plus other products from RealEstateCoach.com. The second section provides information on how to access resources cited in the text. The third section lists additional resources you may find useful in building your business. The fourth section provides a sample Marketing Pledge to use on your listing consultations. For the most up-to-date list of our products and services, visit our website at www.RealEstateCoach.com.

Section 1: Supporting Materials from RealEstateCoach.com

Waging War on Real Estate's Discounters provides you with virtually everything you need to convert your listing appointments into signed business. Mastering the scripts contained in this book will give you a major competitive advantage. To learn the scripts, you can read them from the text or you can select one of the options below:

1. *Waging War Script Cards*
    Many agents find working with script cards is easier than trying to learn the scripts from the text. The cards are available at www.RealEstateCoach.com. To use the cards, select five cards containing the scripts you would like to master. Repeat the scripts out-loud several times a day. For most people, this is all that is necessary to remember them. Once you learn a script, replace it with the card containing the next script you would like to master.

2. *Waging War Scripts on Audio CD*
    A different way to master the scripts is to listen to them on audio CD while you are driving. When you read a script, it can be difficult to determine where to place the emphasis. In contrast, listening to

the materials allows you to learn at a deeper level. The audio CDs are available at www.RealEstateCoach.com.

3. *Seller's Tips Booklet: Who's the Best Person to Sell My House?*
This light-hearted guide for sellers shows how working with a full service broker actually helps the seller net more money. Available in bulk, this is a must-have handout for every listing presentation. Visit our website for more details.

4. *List & Sell Real Estate Like Crazy!* (Audio CD Program)
This program provides you with a systematic approach for converting seller and buyer leads into closed transactions. Topics include how to construct a pre-listing package, dialogues for obtaining the listing at the right price, negotiation scripts and strategies, how to obtain the relocation business, plus two actual listing consultations. The complete buyer's program includes how to conduct a buyer's interview, guidelines for identifying high probability buyers, questioning techniques, offer presentation guidelines, and negotiation strategies. Multiple offer strategies are included for both buyers and sellers as well.

5. *Market & Prospect for Real Estate Like Crazy!* (Audio CD Program)
This program integrates the best real estate prospecting training from the past with the latest 21st Century innovations in technology. The program covers how to create an effective brand, cold calling and door-knocking techniques, detailed strategies for holding a successful open house, how to prospect expired listings and For-Sale-by-Owners, strategies for building a referral network, geographical farming, mailing programs, and how to prospect on the web.

6. *Get Balanced or Get Crazy!* (Audio CD Coaching Program)
This program contains twelve coaching sessions addressing key issues agents face. Topics covered include how to create more time, stress reduction techniques, how to defuse angry situations, knowing when to say "No," how to increase your attractiveness to potential clients, and strategies for increasing profitability including how to move from debt to financial independence.

7. *Coach Your Real Estate Agents Like Crazy!* (Audio CD Coaching Program for Managers)
   This systematic program shows you how to help agents move past what is blocking their performance and get into action now. In five short hours, learn the secrets Master Certified Coaches use to help their clients achieve extraordinary results. This program includes the *Get Balanced or Get Crazy!* Audio CD Coaching Program for agents.

Section 2: Text Resources

Chapter 3: Winning the Psychological War

1. *NAR Publications*
   Realtors® have a strict obligation to avoid price-fixing. For a more detailed discussion of these issues, see the *NAR Code of Ethics* and the *NAR Antitrust Compliance Brochure.*

Chapters 4 and 5: Winning the Agent and Public Campaigns

1. *Contact management systems integrated with complete marketing programs*
   There are a number of excellent mailing programs on the market. Ideally, your contact manager, web prospecting, and your mailing programs are integrated in one program. At the time we went to press, Sharper Agent and Top Producer had the best versions of these programs. To learn more, type the following link into your browser:

   http://realestatecoach.com/technology/contactmgr.html

   To demo the full program, scroll to the bottom of the page and click on "demo."

2. *Virtual tours*
   Most of the top producers interviewed for this book pointed out the importance of producing a high quality virtual tour. To locate the company who does the best job in your area, visit your company's

website as well as websites of your competitors. Note who provides the best quality and then contact the agent to determine who they use. Don't forget to include digital pictures of the property as well.

Chapter 6: Seize the Golden Moment of Opportunity

1. *Call Capture or IVR Technology*
   The two largest companies providing 800 IVR or Call Capture service to the real estate industry are Proquest Technology and ArchTelecom. Our clients at RealEstateCoach.com overwhelmingly prefer Proquest, due in part to the excellent support materials they provide at no additional charge. To learn more about how to use this powerful tool in your business, type the following link into your browser:

   http://www.realestatecoach.com/technology/proquest.html

Chapters 7 and 8: Aim Your Remote Control & Pump Up the Volume

1. *Graphic design*
   Producing a high quality television commercial requires high quality graphics. A great place to locate graphic designers is at www.elance.com. You can pre-screen each designer's work as well as the cost. The designer pays the Elance fee, not the person using the designer's services. A good design will range in price from $250-$700.

2. *Pre-packaged television commercials*
   One of the easiest ways to obtain a television commercial is to sign up with www.e-Agent.biz. e-Agent.biz is a lead generation company, however, they have a separate package for television advertising. Their pre-canned commercials direct viewers to your e-Agent website. This is probably the easiest and least painful way to launch a television ad campaign.

3. *Media advertising kits*
   Regardless of the type of ad you elect to run, where you place your ad is critical. An excellent resource is Thompson Everett. Their free

media kits provide a wealth of information on how to use both radio and television effectively. To learn more visit:

www.thompsoneverett.com/site-map.html

Chapter 9: Kill the Competition with a Killer Website

1. *Website companies*

There are numerous companies competing for your website business. The first decision you must make is whether you want a template site (i.e., a website that offers the same features to numerous agents) or if you want a custom site. A number of our clients are using the Z57.com sites and report having good results with them. Z57 has a team of coaches that assists their users in maximizing their results with their products.

Recently, a new company called VREO Software has arrived on the scene. VREO won the Inman Innovator of the Year Award for 2004. The VREO sites are very professional, but cost a fraction of what a custom site would cost. In addition, VREO has been conducting focus groups to determine the likes and dislikes of today's Internet consumer. Their sites incorporate this feedback into their design so your site and marketing strategies are congruent with what Internet customers want. VREO also provides search engine consulting plus the ability to create a separate URL using the property address for each of your listings.

Other widely used website companies include Advanced Access, A la Mode, and Number 1 Expert. To decide who best fits your needs, look at the features each company provides and how much the service costs. Ask the website company for the URL (web addresses) of several of their clients so you can see how their sites work. If possible, contact the agents to determine whether they are happy with their site and how good the customer service is when there is a problem.

2. *Neighborhood website*

An excellent strategy for becoming the neighborhood expert is to host a neighborhood website. Winner of the Inman Innovator of the Year for 2002, ConnectingNeighbors.com allows agents to start their own neighborhood community website. Neighbors can exchange information and post upcoming events such as birthdays or block parties. The site is a combination of a chat room and a bulletin board. Visitors can also obtain school information, updates on the real estate market, and a host of other pertinent information. ConnectingNeighbors.com monitors the content to minimize the risk of anything inappropriate appearing on your site.

3. *Client website using the property address as the* URL

You have several options in terms of setting up a separate website for sellers. To do it yourself, load your virtual tour to your website and set up a separate link using the property address. Remember to register the address with Network Solutions or one of the companies that registers URLs.

Companies that provide this service are VREO Software and AgencyLogic.com. AgencyLogic.com has a simple template that allows you to set up a website and a brochure in just minutes. They also register the URL for you and in some regions, supply floor plans as well.

4. *Embedded commands*

Chapter 9 introduces the notion of an "embedded command." This term comes from Neurolinguistic Programming (NLP). A number of scripts in *Waging War* use this technique. For example, the script below contains two embedded commands:

Better yet, all I have to do is press a button to activate your website right now and we'll start marketing your property on the web immediately.

The embedded commands are "activate your website right now" and "start marketing your property on the web immediately." The challenge with using embedded commands is that they can be manipulative. To avoid this issue, notice that each of our scripts always turns the decision back to the client.

5. *Agent newsletters*

For years agents have used newsletters to prospect geographical farms and to stay in touch with their sphere of influence. Writing a newsletter can be a daunting chore. A simple solution is to purchase a contact management program such as Sharper Agent or Top Producer that provides a series of postcards, print newsletters, and e-mail marketing campaigns in addition to their contact management tools.

Given the ever-increasing cost of postage, e-mail can be an excellent alternative to using print. While many companies provide high quality e-mail newsletters, our favorite is from MyHomeManagementClub.com. When you meet a potential prospect, offer them a complimentary membership in your Home Management Club. Simply enter the person's e-mail address into the program and the system takes care of the rest. Three times a month your members receive a highly useful newsletter with articles about home improvement, product recalls, home and neighborhood safety, energy conservation, home security, consumer protection, finance and taxes, scam watch, and much more. The newsletter is tailored to fit the geographical location where they live as well as the type of property they live in (single family, condominium, units, or rentals.) The system tracks who opens your e-mails and also helps you to identify who is planning on listing or purchasing. To learn more, type the following URL into your browser:

www.realestatecoach.com/technology/36touch.html

Chapter 10: Rev Up Your Search Engines

1. *Search engine specialists*

Most major website companies provide consulting on how to obtain the best placement on the major search engines. Avoid any company that claims they will list you on hundreds of different search engines. The ones that matter are Google, MSN, and Yahoo. Before hiring a search engine specialist, ask to speak to agents who are using their services. Visit these agent websites and determine how much traffic they receive by examining their Alexa rankings. In addition, type in "real estate" and the geographical area to see whether the agent comes up in a preferred position on the first page of your search.

2. *Pay-per-click programs*

Your search engine specialist can help you with these. You will have to determine how much budget you are willing to allocate to this item. "Pay-per-click" advertising is similar to placing an ad in the newspaper. Normally you have three lines in which to describe your services. Your fee is based upon how many people actually click on your ad. Each time someone "clicks through" to your website, you are charged the amount you agreed to pay. Like print advertising, the more you pay, the better your position. You can set a maximum amount you are willing to pay each month. Again, most large real estate website companies offer this as an additional service to their clients.

3. *Lead generation companies*

At the time this book went to print, HomeGain was by far the largest real estate lead generation company. Their Alexa rankings show they have almost twice as many visitors as compared to any of the major real estate brands. HomeGain offers three different programs. The least expensive is their Agent Evaluator Program. Home buyers and sellers anonymously submit a profile and receive competitive proposals from qualified real estate agents who know their neighborhoods. Buyers and sellers then review the proposals before deciding which agent(s) to contact. They can compare Realtors® prior sales by zip code, current listings, years of experience, commission rates, and more. There is no fee or obligation to the consumer to use the service. HomeGain earns a referral fee from the Realtor® only upon a successful closed transaction.

How it works:

1. You receive real-time buyer and seller leads.

2. You send a personalized response in minutes.

3. Prospects read your response and contact you directly.

HomeGain also provides two other programs for buyers and sellers where you purchase an exclusive area from which you will obtain leads.

There are a number of other lead generation companies including House Values, Lending Tree, Service Magic, and e-Agent.biz. Several of the top-producing agents interviewed for this book use e-Agent.biz as their primary source for lead generation. Also, e-Agent.biz has the extra advantage of providing preproduced television commercials you can use to advertise on cable television.

4. *Alexa.com*

Alexa is owned by Amazon.com and is an objective way to measure web traffic. You can install the Alexa tool bar by visiting www.Alexa.com and clicking on "free tool bar" in the navigation bar. Whether or not you install the tool bar, you can check traffic for other websites by visiting Alexa.com and typing in the URL for the website you want to check.

Chapter 11: Ditch Discounters with a Global Marketing Plan

1. *Relocation*

Virtually all major real estate brands have a relocation company. This service is particularly important if your client is locating outside of your service area. If you work for a small company, joining a lead generation company can also assist you with referrals. When one of your clients is moving outside your service area, you can contact other members of the lead generation company and ask for their assistance. Alternatively, attend NAR regularly to network or join a group like RECyber.com that allows you to post referrals to their members.

2. *Multiple Listing Service in multiple languages*

At the time we went to press, this service was only available through www.Immobel.com. Check with Immobel.com to see if your MLS is already a participant. If so, contact your MLS for instructions for adding the service. If your MLS is not participating, you have two choices. If the service is available in your area, ask your MLS to subscribe. Alternatively, you can subscribe as an individual.

3. *Helpful foreign language resources*
If you work with Hispanic clients, the *English-Spanish Real Estate Glossary* is an excellent resource. This guide defines over 700 real estate terms that are often difficult for non-native speakers to understand. For more information, visit:

http://recenter.tamu.edu/news/70-0603.html

Another resource is the *English-Spanish Real Estate Dictionary* by Olmos and Jacobus, available at your local bookstore or on Amazon.com.

If you want to learn to speak another language, one of the easiest ways is to listen to language tapes while driving. Another strategy it to enroll in a language class at your local college or university.

Many companies now provide services in Spanish. If your company provides this service, make sure you use this in your listing presentation and that you have a link on your personal website.

4. *Marketing $1,000,000 plus estates internationally*
Posting your listings to www.UniqueGlobalEstates.com is a smart strategy, even if you are with a designated estates firm. Because UniqueGlobalEstates.com works only with agents, sellers cannot access this service directly. UniqueGlobalEstates.com is also linked to the DuPont Registry.

Firms that do a substantial amount of estate business may be eligible to join www.LuxuryRealEstate.com. This service is available by invitation only. Have your manager or broker/owner investigate whether your company qualifies to join.

Chapter 12: Setting the Stage for Victory

1. *Feng Shui Resources*
No one understands the real estate business and its relationship to Feng Shui better than Shawne Mitchell (www.ShawneMitchell.com). Her two books on the topic include *Simple Feng Shui: Ancient Principles to Bring Love, Joy, and Prosperity Into Your Life* and *Creating Home Sanctuaries with Feng Shui: Sacred Spaces, Altars, and Shrines.*

2. *Staging your home*

   RealtyTimes.com has a number of excellent articles on staging your home. Once you log on to their site, type in the word "staging" to check the articles in their database on this topic.

Chapter 14: What Your Competitor Fails to Disclose Leaves the Seller Exposed

1. *Making a complete disclosure*

   Because required disclosures vary from state to state, consult your local Board of Realtors® or your department of real estate to determine the requirements in your region. If you work in a litigious area, taking disclosure training as part of your continuing education may be one of the best investments you can make for both your clients and yourself.

2. *Dispute resolution*

   According to the Pepperdine University School of Law, Straus Institute for Dispute Resolution, people are more likely to abide by a decision reached through mediation than when the decision is made by an arbitrator or court of law. Thus, whenever possible, encourage your clients to resolve disputes using a professional mediator rather than filing a lawsuit. If the mediation does not work, the parties can still arbitrate or sue.

Chapter 24: The Ultimate Secret Weapon—the A-bomb

1. *Attraction*

   The attraction principle is a core concept from Coach University's Coach Training Program. The simple model outlined in the text is our version of attraction and has worked effectively for our clients since 1997.

2. *Coach training programs*

   The coaches at RealEstateCoach.com received their formal coach training either from Coach University (www.coachinc.com) or Coaches Training Institute (www.thecoaches.com). Both schools are accredited by the International Coach Federation (ICF). If you're interested in becoming a certified coach, visit www.coachfederation.org. A number of academic institutions now offer coach training, usually within the field of psychology. If you have an interest in becoming a coach or if you are hiring a coach, check credentials. It is fashionable for people to call themselves coaches, even when they lack formal training. The best coaches have been professionally trained by an ICF certified school or a fully accredited college or university.

Section 3: Additional Resources

1. *Free on-line real estate news feed*
    An excellent strategy to keep your website fresh is to use the free news feed from Inman.com. Inman updates the real estate news for your site at no charge. To see how the service works, visit www.Inman.com and click on the tool bar where it says, "Free website content." To sign up, type the following link in your browser:

    www.inman.com/freecontent/index.aspx

2. *Best real estate assessment*
    Are you suited for the business? How do you compare to agents who make at least $150,000 in commissions per year? To learn about your strengths as well as the areas where you need improvement, take the Real Estate IQ test (Real Estate Simulator) on our website by typing the following address in your browser:

    www.realestatecoach.com/featured/simulator.html

3. *Best resource to keep up-to-date with technology*
    Jack Peckham of www.RECyber.com does a terrific job of keeping agents posted on everything from digital cameras to transaction management platforms. RECyber.com provides its members with a complimentary website, complimentary transaction management platform, plus a minimum of at least three interviews per month with industry leaders. They also hold the only on-line real estate conven-

tion each year, free for participants. RECyber.com is one of the best ways to stay current with the technology trends in the industry.

4. *Best software package for real estate agents*

The Real Estate Dashboard (RED) tablet system from Criterion Corporation is designed specifically for real estate agents. It integrates your cell phone and Internet in one place making it simple to check e-mails, call clients back, or fax forms from your tablet PC. The system also has a mapping system to assist you during showings as well as transaction tracking software. The handwriting recognition feature allows you to take notes in the field and then transfer them easily into your database. Coupled with a Tablet PC from Motion Computer or from Toshiba, this is the most technologically sophisticated computer system currently available for today's agent.

Section 4: Marketing Pledge

1. Service to the Clients During the Listing

- Keep all aspects of the transaction confidential.

- Treat clients and their representatives with respect and cooperation.

- Respond to every client call or e-mail within one business day.

- Solicit management assistance immediately if a problem develops.

2. Marketing Services Include

- A written marketing plan listing all websites where the listing will be posted.

- A written advertising and open house schedule.

- A written comparable market analysis that includes current listings, recent sales, plus expired or withdrawn listings.

- A complete document package includes a sample deposit receipt, agency forms, disclosure forms, and an exclusive listing agreement.

3. Processing the Listing

- Complete the full listing packet and turn it in for processing within 24 hours.

- Coordinate sign and key-safe placement.

- Post listing to company website and to Realtor.com as soon as sellers approve the virtual tour and/or digital pictures.

- Place listing on personal web site including color pictures and a detailed description.

4. Servicing the Listing

- Call or e-mail sellers each week with a complete update regarding that week's showings and marketing activities.

- Be present for brokers' opens and all caravans.

- Call or e-mail sellers after all open houses to share feedback.

- Send "Just-listed" cards to neighboring areas.

- Send open house invitations to target area.

- The first week of each month, meet with the seller to review and update the marketing plan, update the comparable sales data, and to discuss positioning with respect to price.

5. Service to Clients During Offer Negotiations

- When possible, present all offers and counteroffers in person.

- While an offer is being negotiated, call or e-mail sellers daily to keep them informed, even if there is no resolution of the negotiation.

- Provide appropriate originals and/or copies of all documents for managerial review as soon as practical and in compliance with the law.

- Assist with financing alternatives.

6. Service to Clients While the Property is Under Contract

- In compliance with the purchase contract, instruct the closing agent/escrow to open and draw documents. Ask closing agent to keep brokers informed directly of all transaction activity.

- Monitor transaction for timely completion of all contingencies including, but not limited to, deposits, inspections, and loan contingencies.

- Arrange for the buyers' inspection appointments.

- If necessary, assist sellers in obtaining estimates for termite and other inspection work.

- Monitor status of buyers' loan and report to sellers.

- Assist sellers in complying with local ordinances that may require installation of smoke detectors, water conservation devices, etc.

- Follow progress of reconveyance deeds and beneficiary statements.

- Monitor progress of buyers' fire and/or flood insurance.

- Anticipate and assist in solving any special problems associated with the sale of the property.

- Coordinate any other transactions relating to the sale of this property.

- Coordinate closing logistics including final closing appointment and moving arrangements.

- Monitor buyers' deposit of funds and signing of all final documents.

- Personally inform sellers when the property has closed/recorded.

- On moving day, transfer keys and garage door openers from sellers to buyers.

- Follow up with sellers to make sure they have received all final documentation.

I look forward to fulfilling my marketing pledge!

Yours Sincerely,

Appendix B: The Agents

We are especially grateful to those agents who volunteered their time and their strategies for this book. If you would like to contact any of the top performers interviewed for this book, you can reach them using the information below.

Craig Ashley
Prudential California Realty, Los Angeles, California
craigashley@earthlink.net
310-207-7080

Tim Burrell
RE/MAX Palos Verdes, California, and
Prudential Carolinas Realty, Raleigh, North Carolina
tim@timburrell.com
310-377-4702

Gail Crann
Keller Williams Realty, Austin, Texas
gcrann@texas.net
512-794-6753

Michael Edlen
Coldwell Banker, Pacific Palisades, California
medlen@coldwellbanker.com
310-230-7373

Ginny Hillenbrand
Burgdorff ERA, Realtors®, Parsippany, Hew Jersey
improvepro@earthlink.net
973-868-4651

Malcolm Kaufman
McGuire Real Estate, San Franscico, California
mkaufman@mcguire.com
415-351-4637

Lee Konowe, Marketing Director
e-Agent.biz, Reston, Virginia
lee@e-agent.biz
703-928-2805

Jackie Leavenworth
Real Estate Coach & Trainer, Cleveland, Ohio
jleavenworth@adelphia.net
216-999-8208

Lucy Matsumoto
Prudential California Realty, Beverly Hills, California
LABuyers.com
310-777-2858

Shawne Mitchell
Village Realtors, Montecito, California
ShawneMitchell.com

Jerry Rossi
RossiSpeaks.com, Raleigh, North Carolina
Speak2Me@RossiSpeaks.com
919-846-6333

Nancy Sanborn
Prudential California Realty, Beverly Hills, California
LABuyers.com
310-777-2858

Don Schoeller
OrlandoRelocation.com, Orlando, Florida
donschoeller@hotmail.com
407-248-8034

Barb Van Stensel
Keller Williams Realty, Chicago, Illinois
ChicagoClassicHomes.com
Phone: 773-564-4268

Adrian Willanger
Windermere Real Estate, Lake Forest Park, Washington
AdrianWillanger.com
adrian@adrianwillanger.com